A Literary Tour Guide to the United States: WEST and MIDWEST

A Literary Tour Guide to the United States: WEST and MIDWEST

BY RITA STEIN

William Morrow & Company, Inc. New York

Library of Congress Cataloging in Publication Data

Stein, Rita.
   A literary tour guide to the United States, West and Midwest.

    Includes index.
    1. Literary landmarks—The West. 2. Literary landmarks—Middle West. 3. Authors, American—Homes and haunts. 4. West—Description and travel—Guide-books. 5. Middle West—Description and travel—Guide-books. I. Title.
PS144.W47S75   917.8′04′3   78-21574
ISBN 0-688-03174-9
ISBN 0-688-08174-6 pbk.

Printed in the United States of America

First Edition
1 2 3 4 5 6 7 8 9 10

To my mother

PREFACE

If there is a theme to this book, it is the spirit of the great westward expansion, the saga of the settlement of the West. The epic of the pioneers, their confrontation with and conquest of the frontier—and the sorrier tale of conflict with Indians who were there before them—is the major theme of American literature of the western United States. Early travelers wrote chronicles of exploration, pioneers left journals and diaries. Their descendants wrote histories, or romances, about the pioneer past, or novels and poems either in praise or in condemnation of the communities that arose out of the empty West. Fortunately, an enthusiasm for historical preservation and a desire to pay tribute to writers both locally and nationally recognized have combined to give us many literary landmarks.

This tour guide directs the traveler and reader to places with literary associations in the midwestern and western United States that are, for the most part, open to the public. Many are authors' former homes, now museums, like Mark Twain's boyhood home in Hannibal, Missouri, or Willa Cather's home in Red Cloud, Nebraska; also included are sites associated with regional writers like Mari Sandoz and Hamlin Garland. Places touched by early chroniclers like Lewis and Clark are also here, as are sites that are the settings for well-known works—from the streets of Sam Spade's San Francisco to the wilds of Jack London's Klondike. Some libraries and museums with exhibits of special interest are in the book as well.

This is not intended to be a work of literary criticism, nor is it a comprehensive literary history. I have, however, provided a brief summary of the literature of each state, focusing mainly on works that are of historical importance or that are by regional

writers who are nonetheless of more than strictly local significance. Titles of books that especially convey the flavor of a particular region or that use a part of the state or a particular city for
a setting have also been suggested, and biographical information
has been provided as background material where appropriate.

For each site, addresses, directions when necessary, and
schedules are given. I have also indicated whether or not there is
an admission charge. If there is one, it will usually be very modest; many places charge under a dollar, with lower fees for children. I have not given exact prices because these frequently
change. A good road map is recommended, especially for getting
to some of the smaller towns. In the directions, SR indicates State
Route. Schedules are subject to frequent alteration and should be
checked before you go.

Since several authors are associated with more than one
place, I have provided cross references within the entries. There
is also an index of authors. Many of the writers mentioned in this
guide also lived in other parts of the country during their
lifetimes. To follow them and to find others the reader is directed
to the companion volumes in this series, *A Literary Tour Guide to
the United States: Northeast,* by Emilie C. Harting, and *South
and Southwest,* by the present author.

Among the many reference works used to gather the information in this volume, the American Guide Series, originally compiled by the WPA Federal Writers' Project and recently revised,
with its chapters on state literatures, has been especially helpful.
*Our Literary Heritage: A Pictorial History of the Writer in
America* (1956), by Van Wyck Brooks and Otto L. Bettman, has
suggested many ideas, as has *Literary America* (1952), a picture
book by David E. Scherman and Rosemarie Redlich. In addition,
The Old West: The Chroniclers, by the Editors of Time-Life
Books with text by Keith Wheeler, is a good, popular illustrated
account of writings about the West.

I am grateful to the many curators, directors, and managers of
these literary sites and to chambers of commerce and city visitors' bureaus for their cooperation in providing valuable information.

R.S.

New York City
July 1978

CONTENTS

CONTENTS

CONTENTS

CONTENTS

CONTENTS

A Literary Tour Guide to the United States: WEST and MIDWEST

ALASKA AND THE YUKON

Early writing about Alaska consisted mostly of narratives of early exploration and of the Russian settlement. The great naturalist John Muir (see Martinez, California) made a trip to the glaciers of south central Alaska in the fall of 1879; his writings about the trip were published in book form only in 1915, under the title *Travels in Alaska*. S. Hall Young, a missionary who traveled with Muir, also wrote a book, called *Alaska Days with John Muir,* published the same year.

The literature of Alaska really started with the great gold rush. After gold was discovered in the Klondike in 1896, thousands of men stampeded into Alaska on their way to the Yukon Territory goldfields. Skagway, Alaska, became the "gateway to the Yukon," and in 1897 and 1898 the hopeful prospectors, with the help of gamblers and outlaws like the notorious Soapy Smith, had made the town "the roughest place on earth." Others passed through Dyea on their way to Chilkoot Pass. In May 1898 construction of a narrow-gauge railroad between Skagway and Whitehorse in the Yukon was begun, and on July 29, 1900, the crews coming from opposite directions met and joined the tracks at Carcross.

The Klondike gold rush furnished writers with many tales of adventure, hardship, tragedy, and triumph; not the least of these writers was Jack London (see also Glen Ellen and Oakland, California). In 1897 he went to the Klondike, having caught the gold fever. He never really got around to mining any gold, but he started writing stories about his experiences in the Klondike, which were published in various magazines. These were collected in 1900 under the title *The Son of the Wolf*. His first novel, *A*

Daughter of the Snows (1902), is set in the Klondike, and the wildness and raw savageness of the Alaskan winter provided him with a fitting background for the most famous of his novels, *The Call of the Wild* (1903), and its sequel, *White Fang* (1905). *Burning Daylight* (1910) and *Smoke Bellew* (1912) are also set in the northern wilderness.

Joaquin Miller (who seems to have showed up almost everywhere at one time or another—see Oakland and San Francisco, California, Hawaii, and Canyon City, Oregon) visited Alaska and the Yukon in 1897 to report on the gold rush for the Hearst papers. In addition to his articles, he wrote a poem called "Alaska." On his return he made appearances on the lecture circuit dressed up in a fur suit with gold nuggets for buttons. His journalistic colleague Hamlin Garland (see West Salem, Wisconsin) went overland into the Yukon Valley in 1898 in search of stories rather than gold, and traveled there for six months. *The Trail of the Gold Seekers* is his account of this trip.

The writer most often linked with the gold rush is Robert W. Service. Born in England, Service went to Canada in 1894 and worked for the Canadian Bank of Commerce in Victoria, British Columbia. He went to the Yukon not as a prospector but as an employee of the bank. He was transferred first to Whitehorse, and then farther north to Dawson, at the confluence of the Klondike and Yukon Rivers, where the first gold strike was made. The **Canadian Imperial Bank of Commerce,** where Service worked from 1907 to 1909, is at First Avenue (Front Street) at Queen Street in **Dawson.** The Gold Room upstairs is open June–Sept., 10–4; free.

Dawson in 1898 was a boom town, the very center of the gold hysteria, filled with suddenly rich prospectors (and many disappointed ones), gamblers, con men, prostitutes, and saloons. Service immortalized this colorful crowd in his humorously melodramatic verse collected under the title *Songs of a Sourdough* (1907), later retitled *The Spell of the Yukon*. The most famous of these ballads are "The Shooting of Dan McGrew" and "The Cremation of Sam McGee." Another collection was called *Ballads of a Cheechako* (1909)—*cheechako* means "tenderfoot" or "newcomer" in the Chinook language. Service also published a novel about the gold rush, *The Trail of '98* (1910). The **cabin that**

Service lived in, reconstructed by Parks Canada, is on Eighth Avenue (open June–mid-Sept.; tours 9–12, 1–6; free); here Service's "ghost" returns daily in summer at 4 p.m. to recite his poetry. On the next block is **Jack London's cabin,** moved to Dawson from its original location on Henderson Creek, where readings of London are given daily in summer at 11 a.m. (free). These historic buildings and others, including an old-time gambling hall, saloons, and a theater, can be seen on city tours during the summer months. Other attractions that conjure up the days that Service chronicled are a "Gaslight Follies" show in the **Palace Grand Theatre** on King Street, and a two-hour cruise on the *Yukon Lou.* For details write Tourism and Information Branch, Government of the Yukon, Box 2703, Whitehorse, Yukon, Canada Y1A 2C6.

The American novelist Rex Beach also came to Alaska in the days of the gold rush. Like London, he did not succeed in striking gold, but he did produce three novels about Alaska, all of them adventure tales: *Pardners* (1905), *The Spoilers* (1906), and *The Barrier* (1907), published together in the omnibus *Alaska Adventures* in 1933. Another early novel of turn-of-the-century boom Alaska is *The Magnetic North* (1904), written by Elizabeth Robins, the feminist actress and playwright, under the pen name she used for her fiction, C. E. Raimond.

In 1976 Congress authorized the establishment of the **Klondike Gold Rush National Park** to preserve what remains of this important era in the history of Alaska. It begins in Seattle, Washington, from where most of the stampeders set off on the voyage to Alaska (Visitor Center at 117 South Main Street, in the Pioneer Square Historic District). **Skagway** is the focal point of the Alaskan part of the park. Here a historic district has been designated that includes boardwalks, false-front buildings, and old stores. There is also a **Trail of '98 Museum.** Skagway is accessible by air from Juneau, Haines, and Whitehorse the year round. Cruise ships stop at Skagway, and the Alaska Marine Highway System provides passage from Seattle via ferry. An automobile access route from Carcross, Yukon, to Skagway was due for completion at the time of this writing. For more information contact Skagway Chamber of Commerce, P.O. Box 194, Skagway, AK 99840, or your travel agent.

The **White Pass & Yukon Route** offers a reasonably priced

railroad trip between Skagway and Whitehorse (now the capital of the Yukon) that follows the Klondike Trail of '98. One of the spots it passes is the area just south of Whitehorse on the Yukon River where Jack London worked for a time as a river pilot. At **Whitehorse,** in the summer, you can take a cruise on the M.V. *Schwatka* through Miles Canyon, the actual place where Jack London piloted his craft, taking prospectors and their outfits to the goldfields. For complete information on this spectacular train trip, write to Manager, Passenger Sales, White Pass & Yukon Route, P.O. Box 2147, Seattle, WA 98111.

Further reading on Alaska: The naturalist John Burroughs made a trip to Alaska in 1899. Unlike the rough conditions of John Muir's 1879 journey, Burroughs's were quite luxurious, since the trip was by boat with the expedition of the financier E. H. Harriman. They went along the Alaska panhandle to Kodiak Island. He reports on this voyage in *Far and Near* (1904).

Alaska-born Barrett Willoughby has written extensively on her native state. Three of her novels with Alaska settings are *The Golden Totem, River House,* and *Sondra O'Moore; Sitka, Portal to Romance* is nonfiction, as is *Alaska Holiday; Alaskans All* and *Gentlemen Unafraid* are collective biographies of outstanding figures in Alaska's history. A number of novels are about the Russian settlement of Alaska in the eighteenth and nineteenth centuries. Stewart Edward White's *Pole Star* is about the Russian fur trade and focuses on Alexander Baranof, founder of the colony at Sitka. Hector Chevigny's *Lord of Alaska* is a biographical novel about Baranof, and Louis L'Amour's *Sitka* is laid in that city in 1867, the year Alaska was purchased by the United States. **Sitka's Centennial Building,** at the harbor, has a model of the town as it looked in 1867; information on historic buildings in Sitka is available at the Chamber of Commerce here. **Sitka National Historic Park** (6 miles north of Sitka; open daily 8–5; closed Thanksgiving, Christmas, New Year's Day) interprets the story of the Russian settlement and also has exhibits on the Tlingit.

Another contemporary novel is Edna Ferber's *Ice Palace* (1958). It was praised more for its local color and background and for its historical material than for its plot and characters, but it does give an interesting picture of Alaska's colorful history. The city of "Baranof" in the book is generally identified as Fairbanks.

Alaska, Alaska, Alaska, a collection of writings about Alaska selected by Helen Hoke, published in 1960, gives a broad spectrum of literature, and includes some Eskimo and native American folk tales and poems. Finally, a beautiful and moving portrait of one man's experiences in modern Alaska is John McPhee's nonfiction book *Coming into the Country* (1977), in which he tells of his encounters with the new pioneers and with "solo" miners, of canoeing on pristine rivers, and of the conflicts between advocates of conservation and of development.

CALIFORNIA

During the period of Spanish and Mexican rule California was little-known territory to English-speaking writers. The most easily accessible book with descriptions of old California is Richard Henry Dana's *Two Years Before the Mast*. Although trappers and explorers, among them Jedediah Smith, had penetrated the area fairly early, it was John C. Frémont who first put firsthand descriptions into print. Frémont, accompanied by Kit Carson, entered California in 1844 after crossing the Sierras from Nevada in midwinter with his exploring expedition. He traversed the region near Lake Tahoe and arrived at Sutter's Fort on the Sacramento River. His report of the expedition, published in 1845 as *Report of the Exploring Expedition to the Rocky Mountains, 1842, and to Oregon and North California, 1843–44* was an instant sensation. In another California expedition in 1845–46 he became involved in the Bear Flag Rebellion against Mexico that ultimately led to the conquest of California. His wife, Jessie Benton Frémont, daughter of Thomas Hart Benton, wrote *Souvenirs of My Time, A Year of American Travel,* and *Far West Sketches,* and in the 1860s was a patroness of the arts in San Francisco. Allan Nevins is the author of the biography *Frémont: Pathmarker of the West,* and Irving Stone's novel *Immortal Wife* (1944) is about the Frémonts.

Clarence King (1842–1901), a geologist, was the first to explore the **Yosemite Valley.** His fine government report on the survey was published in the 1870s, and his *Mountaineering in the Sierra Nevada* (1872; revised edition, 1902), which first appeared in *The Atlantic Monthly,* is a beautifully written book combining scientific observations with vivid description and narrative. *The*

Yosemite by John Muir (see Martinez) is still the best reading for a trip to Yosemite National Park.

California's colorful and exciting history is paralleled by its rich and varied literature. Since the gold rush days, California life has provided writers with unending material. In fact, John A. Sutter, on whose land gold was discovered, although he never benefited from the discovery, was himself the subject of an interesting novel by the French writer Blaise Cendrars called *Sutter's Gold (L'Or, 1925)*. **Sutter's Fort State Historic Park** in **Sacramento** (L St. between 27th and 28th Sts.; daily 10–5; closed Thanksgiving, Christmas, New Year's Day; small admission), is a restoration of the community he established. (Sutter's Mill, where gold was discovered, is at **Marshall Gold Discovery State Historic Site** at **Coloma**.) These writers mined the mother lode of adventure, humor, comedy, and tragedy to be found among the people who came to California to find something better than what they had. In the mid-nineteenth century, Mark Twain and Bret Harte traveled through the Mother Lode country (see Calaveras County) and found themselves working as professional writers in San Francisco, a city that in the twentieth century has continued to be a vibrant center of literary activity. Joaquin Miller (see Oakland) became the poet of the Sierras. Farther south, on the Monterey peninsula, Carmel-by-the-Sea became a famous literary and artistic colony in the early twentieth century. Later, Big Sur, overlooking the Pacific south of Carmel, provided a haven for many writers, including Henry Miller and members of the Beat Generation like Jack Kerouac. More recently, Richard Brautigan has written *A Confederate General from Big Sur*.

Southern California has also been the subject or setting for an enormous number of literary works. Its Spanish past figured in Helen Hunt Jackson's *Ramona,* one of the earliest important works of fiction laid in the region (see Hemet and San Diego). Los Angeles, and especially Hollywood, has, of course, provided twentieth-century writers with endless source material for fiction and drama. *A Literary History of Southern California* by Franklin Walker tells of the early development of literature there.

Two outstanding women writers of the turn of the century made California their home and wrote books about it. Gertrude Atherton (1857–1948) was the author of *The Californians* (1898) and *California: An Intimate History* (1914). Mary Austin, the author of *The Land of Little Rain* (1903), a classic book about the desert of the Southwest, lived in Independence, in the Owens Valley. Her house there has been declared a California historical landmark (not open to the public). Austin wrote *The Ford,* a novel set in the San Joaquin Valley. (Frank Norris's *The Octopus* is about the wheat growers of the same area.)

Two of America's most prominent authors had their roots in California. John Steinbeck was born and grew up in Salinas (which see), and William Saroyan was born and raised in Fresno. Many of Saroyan's stories are about his Armenian relations and friends in that city. One of the country's most prolific authors, Louis L'Amour, makes his home in California and a number of his books on Western subjects are set here, notably *Mojave Crossing* and *The Californios.* Wallace Stegner, a distinguished writer on Western themes, set his novels *Angle of Repose* (1971) and *The Spectator Bird* (1976) in California.

Urban sprawl has obliterated many of the literary landmarks of the state, but a great many are preserved, and where there are no physical remains, you can still retrace the authors' footsteps.

Arcata

In 1857, after a trip to the mining country and a short time working for Wells Fargo, Bret Harte came to Arcata (then called Union), on Humboldt Bay northeast of Eureka, to join his sister Margaret. Here he worked as a typesetter and later a reporter on the weekly local newspaper, *The Northern Californian.* While in residence in the town he lived at **927 J Street.** Although a modern addition was built at this address in 1905, the original smaller house is still part of the structure. It dates from the 1850s and is characterized by clapboard exterior and six-pane double-sash windows (the house is not open to the public).

On February 26, 1860, a small band of white men from nearby Eureka massacred a group of Indians on Indian Island in Humboldt Bay. Harte wrote a scathing editorial in *The Northern*

Californian denouncing this atrocity, saying that "the secrecy of this indiscriminate massacre is an evidence of its disavowal and detestation by the community." Already unpopular for defending minorities, in particular Indians and Mexicans, Harte found it advisable to leave town after the publication of this editorial, which caused much resentment among certain elements in the town. He sailed for San Francisco, where he was to gain fame for his writing. He was twenty-four.

The Arcata Chamber of Commerce, on Seventh Street between H and I Streets, provides a map for a short auto tour of historical spots in Arcata that features nineteenth-century buildings of architectural interest, including the Bret Harte house.

Calaveras County

In *Roughing It,* Mark Twain makes a passing reference to Calaveras County. Toward the end of 1864 Twain had left San Francisco to prospect for gold with a friend, Jim Gillis, at Tuolumne, specifically, at **Jackass Hill** (about halfway between Sonora and Angels Camp along Route 49, one mile west of Tuttletown), where there is now a replica of the cabin he lived in, there for the viewing anytime. Unsuccessful there, they moved on:

> At the end of two months we had never "struck a pocket." We had panned up and down the hillsides till they looked plowed like a field; we could have put in a crop of grain, then, but there would have been no way to get it to market. We got many good "prospects," but when the gold gave out in the pan and we dug down, hoping and longing, we found only emptiness—the pocket that should have been there was as barren as our own.—At last we shouldered our pans and shovels and struck out over the hills to try new localities. We prospected around Angel's Camp, in Calaveras county, during three weeks but had no success.

He may have had no success in finding gold, but it was, at least reputedly, at the bar of the hotel in **Angels Camp** in early

February 1865 that he heard a story about a jumping-frog contest. When he got back to San Francisco, he wrote a story about it called "The Jumping Frog," later known, of course, as "The Celebrated Jumping Frog of Calaveras County." The tale of the frog who loses a jumping contest because it's been filled with quail shot was written in the semiliterate humorous dialect popular during the period. Published in *The Saturday Press* of November 18, 1865, it was a tremendous hit and was reprinted widely. With it Twain gained national fame and, for the first time, critical acclaim.

Angels Camp, one of the historic old towns in the Mother Lode country, is on State Route 49, 12 miles southeast of San Andreas, the county seat. The **Angels Hotel** (at Main and Bird) is a California Historical Landmark. Two miles south of Angels Camp on SR 49 is **"Frogtown,"** the Calaveras County fairgrounds, where every year in late May Twain's story is commemorated with the International Jumping Frog Jubilee (write to Calaveras County Chamber of Commerce, San Andreas, CA 95249 for details).

After leaving Angels Camp Twain went to **Copperopolis** (west of Angels Camp on SR 4), site of the great Union copper mine, which he visited before returning to San Francisco by way of Stockton.

Bret Harte is also, of course, associated with the Mother Lode country. His story "Brown of Calaveras" is set in the area of Angels Camp. Harte had come to the mining country in the mid-1850s and taught school for a time in the town of West Point in Calaveras County. His brief excursion into the mining camps in Calaveras and Amador counties provided him with the lode of local color material that he transformed more than ten years later into his most famous stories, "The Luck of Roaring Camp" and "The Outcasts of Poker Flat," which made him one of the most popular writers of his day.

The area Harte wrote about in his mining camp stories, the **"southern mine district,"** stretches along **Route 49** from Chinese Camp, Jamestown, and Sonora at the south, through Angels Camp and San Andreas, on through Amador City and Drytown (it was anything but) and north to Placerville (formerly called Hangtown), Coloma (with Marshall Gold Discovery State Park), and Auburn. Some of these are ghost towns, some are still thriving communities with restored historic buildings, and you can pan for gold in some places. Remains of gold mines can be seen along the way. **San Andreas** has the **Calaveras County Museum** (30 Main Street; daily except holidays, 9–5 summer, 10–5 rest of year; free), which contains historic exhibits including much material about life during the gold prospecting era. The vestiges of the exciting gold rush past are enhanced by the fact that the region is in the foothills of the Sierra Nevada. The combination of literary resonances, historic interest, and scenic beauty makes this drive very worthwhile.

Calistoga

Robert Louis Stevenson State Park. 8 miles northeast of Calistoga on SR 29. Free.

Robert Louis Stevenson followed Fanny Osbourne to California in 1879, and after waiting in Monterey and then in San Francisco (which see) for her divorce, he married her in San Francisco on May 19, 1880. By then, Stevenson's father had relented in his opposition to his son's behavior and had sent him some money, although finances were still a problem. At the suggestion of a friend, the newly married couple went to Calistoga in the Napa Valley to spend their honeymoon, thinking they could find a vacant old house there left over from the silver mining days. They finally found an abandoned shack at the old Silverado mine, high up on Mount St. Helena, where they lived rent-free for a couple of months. Fanny fixed up the windows and the door, and she and her husband enjoyed the the clean mountain air and the primitive outdoor life, which did much in helping Stevenson to regain his health after yet another serious illness (he was tubercular) in the previous spring. His happy experiences here were later incorporated into *The Silverado Squatters* (1883).

The bunkhouse where the couple spent their honeymoon is no longer standing, but a plaque marks the site where they spent this idyllic interlude. A trail leads up to the site, and there are other hiking trails in the 3200-acre park to an abandoned silver mine and to the summit of the mountain. From the top, in spite of the thick growth of tall trees, which were only small ones a hundred years ago, of course, you can still see as far as San Francisco and the Pacific Ocean on a clear day.

(See also St. Helena for more about Stevenson.)

Carmel

Carmel became a literary and artistic colony before the First World War. In 1905 the poet George Sterling (1869–1926) and his wife Currie came to Carmel and built a house at Tenth and Torres. Other pioneers who came to Carmel with Sterling were the photographer Arnold Genthe and the writer Mary Austin, whose novel *Isidro* has a Carmel setting. Sterling, who had been a protégé of Ambrose Bierce in San Francisco and was part of the Bohemian Club literary circle, invited other writers to visit. Among those who arrived were Bierce, Jack London, and Joaquin Miller. Later, Sinclair Lewis, Upton Sinclair, Lincoln Steffens, and William Rose Benét also spent time here and participated in the lively literary and artistic community that called themselves Bohemians. Many artists and writers took refuge in Carmel after the 1906 earthquake and fire in San Francisco, and a large number stayed, attracted by the artistic ambience and the breathtaking scenery.

The writer most often associated with Carmel is Robinson Jeffers. Jeffers arrived in Carmel in 1914 with his new wife, Una. In 1919 he began building **Tor House** (26304 Ocean View Avenue, at the corner of Scenic Road). Tor House is not open to the public but can be seen from the outside. It is made entirely of granite stones brought up from the beach and was built mainly by Jeffers with his own hands. Next to the house is a tower almost forty feet high, known as Hawk Tower, which Jeffers also built himself from the same sea cobbles as Tor House and which he used as his work place. After completing the tower in 1924, Jeffers began adding rooms to the house, his son helping him with the construction. Jeffers lived in seclusion at Tor House until his death in 1962.

Much of Jeffers's poetry is infused with the spirit and physical beauty of Carmel and the Monterey peninsula, with the rough surf crashing against rocky cliffs and the inland forests, even today mostly still untouched. The tragic narrative "Tamar" is set at **Point Lobos.** "Thurso's Landing" is laid at **Bixby's Landing,** a few miles south on SR 1, and "Roan Stallion" is based on an incident that took place in **Monterey** in which a man was killed by his own horse.

Robinson Jeffers was one of the several young California writers who were recognized and encouraged by George Sterling, and Sterling wrote an appreciation of Jeffers entitled *Robinson Jeffers, the Man and the Artist,* published in 1926.

Carmel also has the historic and beautiful Basilica Mission San Carlos Borromeo, founded by Father Junipero Serra in the eighteenth century. And although present-day Carmel-by-the-Sea is far more wealthy and exclusive than it was in the days before World War I, its artistic heritage lives on in the numerous art galleries and craft shops of the town, which has been strictly zoned to prevent its becoming a honky-tonk. It's not Bohemian anymore (for that, you have to go a bit south to Big Sur), but it is still one of the loveliest towns in California.

Franklin Walker's *The Seacoast of Bohemia: An Account of Early Carmel* (1966) tells of the Bohemian colony of George Sterling and his circle.

Danville

Tao House, former home of Eugene O'Neill. (Not yet open to the public.)

Eugene O'Neill and his third wife, Carlotta Monterey, built this house in 1937 with his 1936 Nobel Prize money, and moved in in late October of that year. Danville is only thirty-five miles from

San Francisco, but it is quite rural. The house is built into the side of a mountain with a magnificent view of the valley below and of a mountain range whose highest peak is Mount Diablo. It has a tile roof, a courtyard, and verandas along the second story. Carlotta filled it with Chinese furniture she bought from Gump's in San Francisco. Arthur and Barbara Gelb in *O'Neill* quote the playwright as saying, "We really have an ideal home with one of the most beautiful views I have ever seen—pure country with no taint of suburbia, and yet we are only fifty minutes' drive from the heart of San Francisco—my favorite American city, although I don't like any city much." They called their home Tao House, *tao* meaning "the right way of life" in Chinese.

O'Neill's years at Tao House were fruitful ones, even though he was plagued by illness. During this period he worked on the never-to-be-finished cycle of plays that included *A Moon for the Misbegotten, A Touch of the Poet,* and the incomplete *More Stately Mansions.* During the summer and fall of 1939 he wrote one of his best plays, *The Iceman Cometh.* And by the end of 1940 he had all but completed his masterpiece, the autobiographical *Long Day's Journey into Night,* which was not to be produced until 1956, three years after the playwright's death. He also planned a series of one-act plays, only one of which, *Hughie,* was completed.

O'Neill accomplished all this in spite of family conflicts (it was in June of 1943 that his daughter Oona married Charlie Chaplin; O'Neill never accepted this marriage and remained estranged from Oona for the rest of his life) and despite deteriorating health. But by the end of autumn 1943, O'Neill's physical condition was so bad (he suffered from a disease similar to Parkinsonism which caused such bad tremors in his hands that he could not hold a pencil to write) that the O'Neills finally decided they would have to leave Tao House and move to San Francisco, where medical attention was more accessible and where Carlotta could be relieved of her heavy housekeeping, nursing, and secretarial burdens. They left reluctantly. The Gelbs quote Carlotta: "We stayed at Tao House for six whole years, longer than we lived anywhere else. Of course, there were many hardships, but it was a beautiful place and I hated to leave." Before they vacated the house in February of 1944 O'Neill destroyed the manuscripts of the first two double-length plays of the cycle and the scenarios of the projected one-acters. But he kept the drafts of some of the other uncompleted plays and the manuscripts of *More Stately Mansions* and of *A Touch of the Poet*.

There are plans to open Tao House as a theater arts center, but money must be raised for renovation and to build a usable access road. At the time of this writing it is *not open to the public*. Tao House was declared a National Historical Site by Congress in 1976. Specially arranged performances of O'Neill plays have already been given here for the benefit of the O'Neill Foundation. For the latest information, contact the Eugene O'Neill Foundation, Tao House, P.O. Box 402, Danville, CA 94526.

Glen Ellen

Jack London State Historic Park. About 8 miles north of Sonoma via SR 12 to Glen Ellen, then 1½ miles west on London Ranch Road. Daily 10–5; trail to ruins of Wolf House closes at 4; closed Thanksgiving, Christmas, and New Year's Day. Small admission.

Jack London was already the famous author of *The Call of the Wild, White Fang,* and *The Sea Wolf* when in 1905 at the age of twenty-nine he began buying land for a farm here in the Valley of the Moon in Sonoma County. He was attracted by the unspoiled beauty of the region and saw in it especially an escape from the urban pressures of living in Oakland (which see). He was divorced from his first wife, Bess Maddern, and in 1905 he married Charmian Kittredge. Together they began to improve what they called Beauty Ranch, buying equipment and building a barn. Their residence in Glen Ellen was interrupted in April 1907 when they decided to make what was intended to be a seven-year voyage around the world on a forty-foot ketch, the *Snark*. Actually, the voyage lasted only twenty-seven months, because London became very ill. Their tour of the South Seas and Australia was later chronicled by London in *The Cruise of the Snark*.

Returning to Glen Ellen in 1909 (the year that the autobio-

graphical novel *Martin Eden* was published), the Londons began
work on Beauty Ranch in earnest. In the next two years they
bought more land and in 1911 moved from town to a small house
on the property. London rode horseback through the hills and
canyons, implemented scientific farming methods, wrote, and in
1911 began planning **Wolf House,** his dream house. His life at
Beauty Ranch with Charmian, a time frequently punctuated by
bouts with alcohol and illness but also a period of great creativity,
is described in Andrew Sinclair's excellent *Jack: A Biography of
Jack London* (1977).

Wolf House was to be a magnificent structure, one that was to
last a very long time. It was to be made entirely of local materials.
Enormous maroon lava boulders drawn in wagons by draft horses
from a quarry three miles away were the basic building stones,
and were blended with redwood logs. The roof was a locally made
dark-red Spanish tile. On the interior there were redwood paneling, concrete walls, nine fireplaces—twenty-six rooms in all, with
a fireproof vault in the basement to house London's papers and
other valuables. It was built at an estimated cost of eighty thousand dollars (it would have cost ten times that in today's money).
This grand and unique home was almost completed when one
August night in 1913 it caught fire. Everything burnable went up
in flames and London was left to contemplate the charred stone
ruins of his dream. Arson was suspected but never proved.

London made remarks to the effect that he would like to re-
build the house, but he never did, instead continuing to live in the
small wood house on the ranch. Overcoming his depression at his
loss, he continued to write. (The 1913 novel *The Valley of the
Moon,* which expresses London's socialist fervor, is set in this
area of Sonoma County.) And he traveled, making trips to New
York, San Francisco, and Los Angeles, sailing on his yawl, the
Roamer, covering the Villa-Carranza troubles in Mexico as a correspondent, and visiting Hawaii (which see). But mainly he continued to devote his time, aside from his writing, to running the
ranch. He was, however, suffering from a number of ailments,
including a kidney condition that was not helped by his drinking,
and he was often in pain. On November 23, 1916, at the age of
forty, he died at the ranch of an overdose of morphine; it may or
may not have been suicide.

From 1919 to 1922 Charmian built the **House of Happy Walls** cn the ranch. It is made of volcanic fieldstone found on the ranch and is surrounded by redwood, Douglas fir, live oak, and madrona trees. Charmian lived here alone until her death at the age of eighty-four in 1955. At her request, she was buried in an unmarked grave on the ranch. In 1959 Irving Shepard, a nephew of Jack London, deeded about forty acres of the original 1500 acres of Beauty Ranch, along with the buildings, to the state of California as a memorial to Jack London. (The state acquired additional acreage later; the park is now about fifty acres.) The House of Happy Walls is a museum of London memorabilia. It contains much of the specially designed furniture that was to have been used in Wolf House. Also on display are London's rolltop desk, an early dictating machine, London's South Seas collection, manuscripts, photographs, and many other mementos of London's adventurous life.

From the House of Happy Walls a hiking trail of about a half mile leads to the ruins of Wolf House. Along the way are eucalyptus trees planted by London. The trail also passes the grave site of Jack London. London was cremated and his ashes were placed here with a simple ceremony. A huge lava boulder, originally intended for use in Wolf House but found to be too large, marks the burial spot, with JACK LONDON carved into it. A bit farther down the road, the ruins of Wolf House, an enormous stone skeleton eerily exposed to the elements, stand as another memorial to one of the most popular American writers of the early twentieth century.

Hemet

Hemet, in the San Jacinto Valley (on Highway 74, southeast of Riverside), lies in the area in which much of Helen Hunt Jackson's novel *Ramona* is set. It was in this inland part of Southern California, where there is a large Indian population, that she did research on the Indians that eventually led her to write her best-selling book. (See also San Diego and Colorado Springs, Colorado.)

Every spring the people of Hemet and the neighboring town of San Jacinto present the *Ramona* outdoor play, a spectacular dramatization of the novel performed in the **Ramona Bowl,** an amphitheater in a canyon on the slopes of Mount San Jacinto. This pageant of old California attracts thousands of visitors and has been presented annually since 1927. Exhibits on Indian lore and handicrafts are on display at the **Ramona Museum** at the entrance to the Ramona Bowl.

For information about tickets write to Ramona Pageant Association, P.O. Box 755, Hemet, CA 92343.

Los Angeles

The sprawling group of "suburbs in search of a city" known as Los Angeles has not so much inspired as provoked scores of works of fiction and drama. Because Southern California has attracted many eccentrics, and because of the crazy, flamboyant movie colony, Los Angeles seems to have lent itself especially to satire. Jeremy Pordage's entrance into Los Angeles in Aldous Huxley's *After Many a Summer Dies the Swan* (1939), with his drive past palm trees, old ladies in crimson pants, filling stations, billboards, cocktail lounges, cemeteries, restaurants in the shape of bulldogs, and mansions that look like Tibetan lamaseries, is classically evocative of the delightful vulgarity that was L.A. in the thirties (and to some extent still is today). The unbelievable Forest Lawn cemetery in Glendale inspired Evelyn Waugh to write his hilarious satire on American funeral practices, *The Loved One*.

Hollywood has been grist for the writer's mill since D. W. Griffith moved west. Novelists have particularly favored exposing the seamy side of the "glamour capital of the world" and portraying sadness and disillusionment behind the glossy façade. *The Day of the Locust* (1939) by Nathanael West is a powerful novel about the failure of the American dream as epitomized by the losers of Hollywood. Its apocalyptic riot scene takes place in front of a theater not unlike **Mann's** (formerly Grauman's) **Chinese Theater** on Hollywood Boulevard. F. Scott Fitzgerald's last novel, incomplete at the time of his death in Hollywood in 1940, was *The Last Tycoon*, which is about a young and rich Hollywood producer resembling the legendary Irving Thalberg. Budd Schulberg, whose novel *The Disenchanted* is based on Fitzgerald's declining years, is also the author of one of the most famous of Hollywood novels, *What Makes Sammy Run?* (1941), about the rise of Sammy Glick from the streets of New York to power as a movie mogul. Clifford Odets's play *The Big Knife* also deals with the brutal realities of Hollywood, and so does Norman Mailer's *The Deer Park.*

Two of the best writers of hard-boiled crime stories used Los Angeles as a locale. James M. Cain's *Mildred Pierce* (filmed with Joan Crawford) is set in Glendale, a Los Angeles suburb. Raymond Chandler's detective hero Philip Marlowe explored the underside of L.A. in *The Big Sleep, Farewell, My Lovely, The Long Goodbye,* and other stories. One of the finest evocations of contemporary Los Angeles life is Joan Didion's *Play It As It Lays,* whose heroine incessantly drives the freeways trying to escape her anomie.

There is, however, another, historical aspect to Los Angeles, interpreted at **El Pueblo de Los Angeles State Historic Park** in downtown L.A., where buildings from the nineteenth-century Mexican settlement have been restored. One man who would have been pleased at this preservation was Charles F. Lummis:

Charles F. Lummis Memorial Home State Historical Monument. 200 East Avenue 43, 5 miles north of central Los Angeles off the Pasadena Freeway (SR 11), exit Avenue 43, in Highland Park section. Daily except Sat. and certain holidays, 1–4. Free.

Charles F. Lummis (1859–1928) was an author and historian who devoted most of his life to the study and preservation of Indian and Spanish traditions and artifacts of the American Southwest and especially of Southern California. As a young man of twenty-five he walked to Los Angeles from Ohio. He became a reporter for the Los Angeles *Times,* and was city editor of that newspaper from 1885 to 1887. Los Angeles at that time was a city in the middle of a real estate boom and at the beginning of an influx of immigrants from other parts of the country and from abroad that has not stopped yet, almost a hundred years later.

Lummis made many expeditions through the Southwest, lived among the Pueblo Indians from 1889 to 1891, and went on an ethnological expedition to Peru and Bolivia (1892–1894). He was the author of a number of books on the history, archaeology, and people of these regions, among them *The Spanish Pioneers; Mesa, Cañon and Pueblo;* and *The Land of Poco Tiempo.*

Lummis founded the magazine *The Land of Sunshine* (later called *Out West*) in 1894 and edited it until 1910. By publishing talented California writers like Joaquin Miller, Jack London, Edwin Markham, Robinson Jeffers, and Frank Norris, he helped bring about the recognition of California as a vibrant new cultural center of the country. He also promoted the cause of preserving the old Spanish missions of California and other historic relics, and was a champion of Indian rights. Especially able as a promoter of the attractions of sunny Southern California, he was the originator of the slogan "See America first." From 1905 to 1910 he was the director of the Los Angeles Public Library.

In 1897, on a site he had chosen in 1895, Lummis began building this house, which he called **El Alisal** (the Sycamore), because a gigantic sycamore stood here (it has since died and four saplings grow in its place). He built this two-story-high castlelike home largely with his own hands from stones found on the property and along the banks of the nearby Arroyo Seco. It has thirteen rooms and measures ninety feet from east to west. It is solidly built of granite and concrete, and Lummis, who worked on it for fifteen years, meant it to last so that future generations could share the exhibits that he had gathered as an explorer, historian, and archaeologist. Even during his lifetime, Lummis displayed his collections of artifacts from the Southwest and from Central and South America in the museum area to the right of the entrance hall. Lummis also arranged concerts, lectures, and other entertainments for friends here. Will Rogers joked and did his rope tricks, and Madame Schumann-Heink sang here. The house also contains Lummis's office, the dining room (or *comedor*), and a kitchen (the *cocina*) modeled after one in a California mission. Famous visitors included the California author Mary Austin,

Blasco Ibáñez, John Burroughs, Carl Sandburg, and many other notables. Lummis's circle was wide; it emcompassed not only other literary people, but artists, musicians, actors, scientists, political figures, and many Spanish and Indian friends, and their photographs decorate the walls of El Alisal. Lummis died in 1928; his ashes are sealed within the wall of the patio portal. (The Lummis Home is the headquarters of the Historical Society of Southern California.)

One of Lummis's lasting achievements was the founding of the **Southwest Museum** (234 Museum Drive at Marmion Way, a little north of the Lummis Home; daily except Mon. 1–4:45; closed mid-Aug.–mid-Sept.; free). The museum has an impressive collection of artifacts of American Indians, with a special emphasis on the Native Americans of the southwestern United States.

Will Rogers State Historic Park. 14253 Sunset Boulevard, Pacific Palisades. Daily except Thanksgiving, Christmas, and New Year's Day; park open 8–5, house 10–5. Fee for car, free for walk-ins.

Will Rogers, born in Oklahoma, began his career as a trick roper in traveling Wild West shows, and he ultimately became a star in the Ziegfeld Follies as a comedian and raconteur. His first sojourn in Hollywood, beginning in 1919, was only moderately successful, and after about three years he returned to the stage. It was only after talkies came in that he became as hugely successful in films as he had been in live performances. Meanwhile, he also became an enormously popular writer with a syndicated column that had a readership in the millions. His humorous commentaries on the political and social foibles of the American people appeared in newspapers throughout the country, and he was also the author of a number of books, including *The Cowboy Philosopher on Prohibition* (1919), *The Illiterate Digest* (1924), *Letters of a Self-Made Diplomat to His President* (1926), and *Ether and Me or Just Relax* (1929). His writings, his movies, his stage and radio appearances, all flavored with his famous good-natured wit and homespun modesty, made him one of the most beloved personalities in America, and his death in an airplane crash in Alaska with Wiley Post on August 15, 1935, was a great shock not just to America but to the world.

Rogers built this house on his ranch in 1928, converting a cabin he had used on weekends into the living room of his home. This high-ceilinged living room is filled with some of Rogers's collection of Indian artifacts, blankets, sombreros, cowboy items, and a mounted steer head over the fireplace. (The Will Rogers Memorial, in Claremore, Oklahoma, has a more extensive collection of Rogers memorabilia.) The room actually did not contain such a varied collection of items when Rogers lived here, but was arranged this way by Mrs. Rogers after Will's death when she opened the house for tours to benefit the Red Cross.

Otherwise the grounds and buildings are maintained as they were when the Rogers family lived here. The ranch was presented to the state of California in 1944, after the death of Mrs. Rogers. The grounds include a stable, a riding ring, corrals, and a roping arena. Polo ponies are kept in the stable and polo matches are still held on the polo field where Rogers used to play. In the wooded hills around the house are the riding trails laid out by Rogers, still in use.

The Huntington Library. 1151 Oxford Road, San Marino, 12 miles northeast of downtown Los Angeles via Pasadena Freeway. Tues.–Sun. 1–4:30; closed Mon., major holidays, and month of October. Gardens open at 10:30 a.m. Free.

The Huntington Library, with its collection of over half a million books and five million manuscripts, serves scholars from all over the world. Its holdings of rare books and manuscripts in the fields of American and English literature and history are among the finest in existence and are housed in a handsome neoclassical marble building. In the **Main Exhibition Hall** almost two hundred items from the collections are on permanent display. These include a Gutenberg Bible, the Ellesmere manuscript of Chaucer's *Canterbury Tales* dating from 1401, first printings of Shakespeare's plays, a magnificent fifteenth-century book of hours, autograph manuscripts of important English and American literary works, engravings by William Blake, and many more treasures. There are also special changing exhibitions of other manuscripts and books in rooms adjacent to the Main Hall.

The library building also houses part of the art collection, but the major part is in the separate **Art Gallery,** formerly the palatial home of the founder, Henry E. Huntington, a short distance from the library. The collection is primarily of British art of the eighteenth and nineteenth centuries, and includes two of the most famous of English paintings, Gainsborough's *Blue Boy* and Lawrence's *Pinkie*. There are also works by Reynolds and Constable, among others.

The library and Art Gallery are surrounded by acres of beautiful gardens: a Japanese Garden, a Rose Garden, the Camellia Collection, the Palm Garden, and the Desert Garden. Of special interest is the Shakespeare Garden, northwest of the Art Gallery, an acre of plants and flowers (in season) used in Elizabethan gardens, many of them mentioned in Shakespeare.

Martinez

John Muir National Historic Site. 4202 Alhambra Avenue, just off SR 4, Alhambra Avenue exit. Daily except Thanksgiving, Christmas, and New Year's Day, 8:30–4:30. Small admission; under 16 and over 61 free.

John Muir, the great naturalist and conservationist, was born in Scotland in 1838, and came to America in 1849 with his family. They settled on a farm they had hewn out of the wilderness near Portage, Wisconsin (which see). Young John did arduous chores that the farm demanded, but also found time to read and to invent numerous mechanical devices. He tells of his early years in *The Story of My Boyhood and Youth* (1913). He went to the University of Wisconsin but left without taking his degree. His interest in the natural sciences led him to take extensive walking trips throughout the Midwest and Canada, during which he studied the botany and geology of the region firsthand. An eye injury in 1867 led him to abandon his work on mechanical inventions and he decided to spend the rest of his life studying nature, the "inventions of God." He walked from Indiana to the Gulf of Mexico; his journal of this trip was published in 1916 as *A Thousand-Mile Walk to the Gulf.* In 1868 he traveled to the Yosemite Valley, and he later headed out to the Pacific Northwest and Alaska to study glaciers. During his lifetime he made treks through wilderness areas in many parts of the globe—South America, Africa, Asia, Australia—often traveling with other scientists and naturalists, including John Burroughs. He collected botanical specimens on these travels, and made a specialty of the study of trees.

Muir began writing articles on behalf of the preservation of wilderness areas and natural resources in the 1870s, and urged the establishment of national parks and forest preserves. His advocacy of conservation came to real fruition during the next thirty years with the founding of the United States Forest Service, the opening of Yosemite, Sequoia, and Mount Rainier National Parks, the establishment of forest reserves, the designation of the Grand Canyon as a national monument, and the saving of other national treasures of natural beauty. In 1903 he persuaded President Theodore Roosevelt to support the preservation of millions of more acres of forests and parks in order to protect them forever from commercial exploitation. He was also one of the founders of the Sierra Club in 1892.

Although Muir wrote for magazines and newspapers in the 1870s and 1880s, his first book was not published until 1894. This was *The Mountains of California,* which evinced not only his devotion to the cause of conservation but a poetic literary style as well. Other works followed: *Our National Parks* (1901), *Stickeen* (1909), a tribute to his little half-wild dog, *The Yosemite* (1912), and other records and journals of his travels, all of which combine the precise observations of a naturalist with the sensitivity and style of a fine writer.

Muir settled here on the ranch in Martinez when he married the daughter of Dr. John Strentzel, who had emigrated from Poland in 1849. Dr. Strentzel had been a horticulturist as well as a physician, and had developed extensive fruit orchards on his land. During the first ten years of his marriage, Muir was extremely successful at growing fruit. Using his knowlege of botany, he created new varieties of pears and grapes. He did so well that after this first decade he was able to retire from the business and turn it over to a foreman to run so he could devote his full time to his travels, studies, and writing. A fragment of the original orchards is preserved on the present nine-acre site. In between his trips he came back to this house to write his many books and articles. His writings had a profound effect on how the American people think about their natural environment, and they can also stand independently as literary works.

Muir died in Los Angeles on December 24, 1914. On his death the original furnishings of the seventeen-room Victorian mansion that was his home were removed. The National Park Service is refurnishing the home in the style of the period of 1906–14, and most of the rooms now reflect the life Muir lived here in this comfortable home.

The **Martinez Adobe,** which was built in 1849, is down a road through the orchard and can be reached by walking along the Orchard Trail near the main house. It was used as a foreman's residence and later as the home of Muir's daughter Wanda and her husband. It is open on weekends from 1 to 4. It is not furnished, but changing exhibits on California history are on display.

A documentary film about the accomplishments of John Muir is shown on the hour at the Visitor Center, and publications by and about Muir are on sale. Tours of the home are self-guiding, but guided tours are available daily at 10:30 and 2:30.

Monterey

From a literary standpoint, Monterey is probably best known as the locale of John Steinbeck's novels about poor Mexican-American paisanos: *Tortilla Flat, Cannery Row,* and *Sweet Thursday.* Monterey has changed considerably since the days when these stories take place, but some of the locations are still identifiable. The Church of San Carlos in *Sweet Thursday* is **San Carlos Cathedral** on Church Street. The canneries that arose because of Monterey's importance as a fishing and whaling center are no more, but the wharf still has its share of fishing boats.

Cannery Row has been transformed into a street of restaurants, boutiques, and art galleries (there is a bronze bust of Steinbeck at Cannery Row and Prescott). The **Pacific Biological Laboratories** (called Western Biological Laboratory in Steinbeck's work) at 800 Cannery Row, now a private social club, were owned by Steinbeck's good friend "Doc" Edward Ricketts, a marine biologist whose philosophical thought influenced Steinbeck. "Doc's Lab" appears in *Cannery Row, Sweet Thursday, Travels with Charley,* and *The Sea of Cortez.* Steinbeck owned and lived in the house at 460 Pierce, the **Casa Jesus Soto Adobe** (built in 1842) during the 1940s (it is not open to the public). Steinbeck is, of course, associated with the entire Monterey peninsula, where parts of the above-mentioned books are set. He spent vacations during his boyhood in Pacific Grove and later lived in a small house there during his first marriage. (See Salinas for more about Steinbeck.)

Monterey has a colorful history that begins with the discovery of Monterey Bay in 1602 by the Spanish explorer Sebastian Vizcaino and includes rule by Spain, Mexico, and finally the United States after the Mexican War, when the American flag was raised over the city in 1846. A **"Path of History,"** indicated by a red line down the center of certain streets, directs the visitor to historic homes and buildings in Monterey, many of which date back to Spanish and Mexican days, and all of which have plaques explaining their significance. Many of these buildings are part of the Monterey State Historic Park, a group of restored buildings of especial historic and architectural importance. (Most buildings are open daily 9–5 except Thanksgiving, Christmas, and New Year's Day. A ticket is available for a small fee at any of the sites and is good for all buildings.) Two of these structures are of particular literary interest: the Robert Louis Stevenson House and California's First Theatre.

Robert Louis Stevenson House. 530 Houston Street. Daily 9–5. 45-minute guided tours hourly.

Robert Louis Stevenson was in Monterey from early autumn 1879 to mid-December of that year. He had crossed the Atlantic and then the American continent on an emigrant train, a voyage he later recorded in *The Amateur Emigrant,* in order to follow Fanny Osbourne, a married American woman with whom he had fallen in love in France in 1876. Fanny's marriage was falling apart and she was in the process of getting a divorce. She had come down to Monterey from her home in Oakland for a short stay that had lengthened into a rather long one, and with her were her two children, Lloyd and Belle, and her sister Nellie, who subsequently married a young Monterey man of Spanish stock, Adolfo Sanchez.

When Stevenson arrived in Monterey he was tired, ill, and practically penniless, financial help from his disapproving parents having been cut off. After a disastrous attempt at camping in the nearby woods, during which he fell ill and had to be rescued by an old woodsman, he moved into an old adobe building which was then known as Girardin's French House, now the Robert Louis Stevenson House. The house, the original part of which dates from the 1830s, had been acquired by Juan Girardin, a Frenchman, in 1856. He and his wife made some additions and rented out rooms. Stevenson occupied an airy room on the second floor. While waiting for Fanny to obtain her divorce, Stevenson lived here, made several friends, and wrote. He made special friends with Jules Simoneau, an old Frenchman at whose restaurant he took many of his meals. He also made the acquaintance of a Mr. Bronson, editor of *The Monterey Californian,* the local newspaper, who paid Stevenson two dollars a week to write for the paper. Actually, this money was more an act of charity, contributed by other habitués of Simoneau's restaurant when they saw the penury in which Stevenson was living. Stevenson did, however, produce some articles, including "The Old Pacific Capital," a picture of Monterey at that period. In spite of his frail health and his impatience and uncertainty about Fanny's divorce, he grew to love Monterey, enjoying its pleasant climate and the sound of the sea. He describes his sojourn here in positive terms in several of his letters. But meanwhile, Fanny had had to return to Oakland, and when Stevenson had recovered from an attack of pleurisy, he went north to San Francisco (which see), where he waited, most of the time ill, until May of 1880, when he finally was able to marry Fanny.

The Stevenson House in Monterey has been restored as a home of the period of the 1870s, and several rooms in the house are devoted to an exhibit of Stevensoniana. (See also Calistoga and St. Helena.)

First Theatre. Corner of Scott and Pacific Streets. Daily except Mon. 9–5. Performances throughout the year; inquire for schedule.

California's first theater started out in 1847 as a boardinghouse built by Jack Swan, who had come from England and settled in Monterey in 1843. To attract lodgers, he set up a barroom on the premises. A company of soldiers stationed in Monterey in 1847 (it was shortly after the Mexican War) decided to put on a play to relieve the boredom of their duty. Swan's building had a suitably large room and he furnished it with a stage, benches, lamps, and candle footlights. The curtains were improvised from some blankets. Some of the first productions were such masterpieces as *Putnam, the Iron Son of '76; Box and Cox;* and *Nan, the Good-for-Nothing,* but some scenes from *Romeo and Juliet* were also presented (how they were performed one shudders, or laughs, to imagine). On the first night seats went for five dollars, an enormous sum in those days, and the house was sold out.

The building was given to the state of California in 1906 as a monument. Early theatrical programs and other memorabilia are on display, and the theater is still used for productions of nineteenth-century plays for the edification of the theatergoing public.

Nevada City

Nevada Theatre. 401 Broad Street. In use throughout the year for plays, lectures, and other events.

Nevada City, called the "Queen City of the Northern Mines," was a boom town during the gold rush. From a tiny mining camp in 1849 it grew in the 1850s and 1860s, in spite of a series of fires, to be one of the most prosperous and important of the mining towns of northern California, and many of the fine Victorian homes built here by people who made mining fortunes still stand, as do two hotels from that era, the National and the New York.

Money also brought a desire for culture and entertainment. The Nevada Theatre, built from the bricks of the old Bailey

House Hotel, opened September 9, 1865, making it California's oldest existing structure built specifically and exclusively as a theater. It had a forty-five-foot stage and gas footlights, and was quite a magnificent edifice for the time and place. What makes it especially notable as a literary landmark is the fact that Mark Twain lectured here shortly after its opening. In October 1865 he spoke about his trip to the Sandwich Islands (Hawaii, which see) on his first lecture tour. The local newspaper reported that he charmed his audience. Jack London also spoke from the stage of the Nevada Theatre in 1910.

In 1915 the building became a movie theater, but it closed in 1958 and was left in a forlorn state. Through the fund-raising efforts of the Liberal Arts Commission of Nevada City, the theater was purchased and restored; it reopened in 1968 to serve the cultural needs of the city. It has been declared a California Historical Landmark.

Oakland

Oakland, across the bay from San Francisco, has a number of literary associations. Richard Henry Dana, author of *Two Years Before the Mast,* probably hung out around the waterfront with the crew of the *Pilgrim,* on which he made his famous voyage in 1834. Robert Louis Stevenson, living in San Francisco in the first half of 1880, visited his fiancée Fanny Osbourne in her Oakland cottage, making the trip across the bay by ferry. (They were married in May 1880. See Calistoga, Monterey, St. Helena, and San Francisco.) Later, in 1888, he watched at the Oakland waterfront as his schooner, the *Casco,* was prepared for their voyage to the South Seas (see Hawaii).

Bret Harte spent part of his youth in Oakland. Harte's mother, a widow, went to California in 1853 and married Colonel Andrew Williams of Oakland. When Harte followed her out to the West Coast in 1854 he lived during different brief periods in his stepfather's house, supporting himself at a variety of jobs, including teaching, before he left for Union, California (now Arcata, which see). The **Bret Harte Boardwalk** (in the 500 block of Fifth Street, six blocks east of Jack London Square; see below) is a row of

restored Victorian homes converted into boutiques and restaurants across the street from where Harte lived. The **Colonel Star-
bottle** bar, named after one of Harte's characters, has an authentic portrait of Harte's stepfather, the model for the character, and
Roaring Camp Mercantile, one of the shops, has a sign about
Harte's connection to the neighborhood.

Jack London Square, at the foot of Broadway (from San Francisco take Bay Bridge and Nimitz Freeway, SR 17, to
Broadway-Alameda exit), is a group of restaurants and other
buildings at the waterfront of the Oakland estuary. This area had
fallen into ruin and disrepair, but under the guidance of the Oakland Board of Port Commissioners, it was rescued from total
neglect and transformed into a beautiful convention and tourist
center; it was dedicated in 1951 and has grown considerably since
then. In the center of the square is a statue of London with a
commemorative plaque.

Jack London spent much of his youth in Oakland. Although
born in San Francisco, London soon moved to Oakland, where he
led quite a wild adolescence. Born in poverty, he quit school
when he was fourteen and soon became known as the king of the
oyster pirates. He and his gang would raid the oyster beds along
the beach and sell their booty along the waterfront. Later he got
his own boat, went straight, and even worked for the law, as he
recounts in *Tales of the Fish Patrol* (1905). He also had his quieter
moments, though, some of which he spent in the Oakland Public
Library, where he was guided in his reading by the poet Ina
Coolbrith (see San Francisco), who was the librarian from 1874 to
1893.

London's favorite hangout on the waterfront was **Heinold's
First and Last Chance** (foot of Webster Street), a saloon in a shack
that had originally been used as a bunkhouse for oystermen.
Heinold's is the only building Jack London would recognize on
Jack London Square if he were to come back. Johnny Heinold
opened his saloon in 1883 after he purchased the shack for a
hundred dollars. London writes of Heinold in *John Barleycorn*
(1913), his autobiographical work that is also a tract against drinking, a weakness with which he was afflicted throughout his life.
He writes that "it was Johnny Heinhold [London's misspelling]
who secretly warned me across the bar that I was getting
pickled," and then goes on to describe his drinking exploits there

and the camaraderie of the men who patronized the place. Joaquin Miller and Robert Louis Stevenson were also patrons at various times.

London later returned to Oakland when he was a famous author to supervise the building of the *Snark,* the ketch he sailed to the South Pacific in 1907 (see Glen Ellen).

Also on Jack London Square is the **Sea Wolf** restaurant (a new building), which has a collection of photographs of Jack London. Nearby on **Jack London Mall** is a cabin London used during his winter in the Klondike (see Alaska), brought down to Oakland for display. Just south of Jack London Square is **Jack London Village,** an attractive new complex of boutiques and shops built around a series of boardwalks and ramps, with two restaurants on the waterfront.

Joaquin Miller also left his mark on Oakland. After an adventurous life that began with his running away to the goldfields at the age of seventeen and included living with the Indians, running a pony express in Washington territory, schoolteaching, editing a newspaper, and being a judge (see Canyon City, Oregon), then being lionized in London as the "poet of the Sierras" and living abroad for many years, Miller returned to the United States. In 1886, at the age of forty-seven, he settled in Oakland in the hills above the town on an estate he called **The Hights** (his spelling), which is now **Joaquin Miller Park** (at Joaquin Miller Road via Warren Freeway; daily 9 a.m.–11 p.m.; free), run by the city of Oakland. In this wilderness area he planted eucalyptus and other trees that are now a forest. His wife, his mother, and his daughter lived with him at The Hights, where each had a separate cottage so that his ideas about the need for solitude could be properly fulfilled. His own small house, called The Abbey, still stands on the site, as do three stone monuments Miller built to Moses, Robert Browning, and John C. Frémont. He also built a funeral pyre that was to be used at his death (it never was).

Miller was always something of a poseur—in London in the 1870s he wore chaps, fancy boots, and a sombrero indoors and out to perpetuate his image as a Westerner—and the exaggerated romanticism of his poetry reflects his personality. When he took up residence at The Hights he continued to live as he had done, advocating the simple life and maintaining his image as a bearded sage and eccentric. He would write in bed in the morning, listening to raindrops pattering on the roof, raindrops produced by a contraption of perforated pipes he had rigged up because the sound "inspired" him. He covered himself with animal skins instead of blankets, since this was more "natural" and "primitive." Many people came to visit and pay homage, and not only The Hights but Miller himself became somewhat of a local landmark. He died here in 1913, and although his funeral pyre was not used, he *was* cremated, and in accordance with his wishes, his ashes were scattered in the High Sierras.

St. Helena

The Silverado Museum. 1347 Railroad Avenue. Daily except Mon. and holidays, 12–4. Free.

The Silverado Museum, housed in an 1884 stone building called The Hatchery, contains one of the largest collections of items relating to Robert Louis Stevenson in the world. The name of the museum derives from the site on Mount St. Helena (eighteen miles north; see Calistoga) where Stevenson and his bride, Fanny, spent their honeymoon in 1880 and where he wrote the first draft of *The Silverado Squatters.*

The Silverado Museum is sponsored by the Vailima Foundation, named after Stevenson's last home in Samoa. It was founded by Norman Strouse, a noted bibliophile, who bought land in St. Helena and dreamed of establishing a museum to display his collection of Stevensoniana. The museum opened its doors on December 14, 1969, seventy-five years after Stevenson's death. On display are more than two hundred Stevenson items and a number of paintings, although the museum actually houses over 4500 catalogued items available to scholars. Among the things on exhibit are rare first editions, autograph manuscripts and letters, books from Stevenson's library, personal items including some of his childhood toys, and family photographs. The writing desk Stevenson used at Vailima and other items from his Samoa plantation can also be seen.

Salinas

Salinas is the heart of Steinbeck country. John Steinbeck was
born in 1902 in what is now known as the **Steinbeck House** (132
Central Avenue). A Victorian structure with a turret and ginger-
bread decoration, it is now operated as a luncheon restaurant by
the Valley Guild, with profits used for renovation and mainte-
nance of the house and for charity. Steinbeck memorabilia are
displayed around the house, and a basement shop, "The Best
Cellar," sells his books and handcrafted items. (Steinbeck House
is open Mon.–Fri.; two seatings, at 11:45 and 1:15; reservations
required: telephone 408-424-2735; group tours can be arranged.)

Steinbeck grew up in Salinas and went to the local high
school, from which he graduated in 1919; his first published work
appeared in *El Gabilan,* the high school paper. Although he went
to Stanford University, he dropped out without graduating. He
preferred to work with the ranch hands and migrant workers in
the Salinas Valley, and the people he met and the experiences he
had became an integral part of his fiction. Salinas and the surrounding countryside are rich in places associated with Steinbeck.

In Salinas, in addition to the birthplace, there is the **John
Steinbeck Library** (110 West San Luis Street). Steinbeck did research for *East of Eden,* which is set in Salinas, in the old wing.
The library has a Steinbeck Room with photographs, first editions, manuscripts, and memorabilia on display. The **South Main
Street** area downtown is being revitalized. Here and in other parts
of the city there is much interesting Victorian architecture, some
in the Queen Anne style, that is being restored and preserved.
The **East of Eden Restaurant** (327 Pajaro Street; open 7 days a
week) is in an old converted Presbyterian church that appears in
East of Eden.

Steinbeck's grave is in the **Garden of Memories** (768 Abbott),
in the Hamilton plot under the large oak closest to Romie Lane.
His maternal grandparents, Samuel and Elizabeth Hamilton, and

some other relations who are mentioned in *East of Eden,* are also buried in this cemetery.

The **Salinas Valley,** stretching southeast of Salinas (drive along US 101) is the locale for *Of Mice and Men* (set on a ranch a few miles south of Soledad), *The Red Pony,* parts of *East of Eden,* and several short stories. Other Steinbeck sites are west of Salinas toward Monterey and the Pacific (see Monterey). An excellent booklet describing four one-day self-guided tours entitled *Steinbeck Country Starts in Salinas* (50¢) is available from the Salinas Chamber of Commerce, 119 East Alisal, Salinas, CA 93901.

San Diego

Old Town San Diego. From downtown San Diego take SR 5 northwest to Old Town Avenue.

In 1882 Helen Hunt Jackson was appointed by the federal government as a special commissioner for the Bureau of Indian Affairs to investigate the conditions of Indians in California. Her appointment had come after she wrote *A Century of Dishonor* (1881), a long tract setting forth in great detail how the Indians had been betrayed and cheated by the United States Government since the establishment of the country. She had sent each member of Congress a copy of this report at her own expense.

When Jackson came to California in 1882 she was a guest at the Estudillo home on San Diego Street, now restored and known as **La Casa de Estudillo** (built 1829), which is part of Old Town San Diego State Historic Park (house open daily, May–Sept., 10–6, rest of year to 5; closed Thanksgiving, Christmas, New Year's Day; small admission). Here and elsewhere in Southern California, in particular at the Camulos ranch—called the Moreno ranch in *Ramona*—near Ventura, and in the Indian country around Hemet (which see), she gathered material for her novel *Ramona* (1884), which was an instant success when it was published. (The Camulos ranch is now the Del Valle ranch—private; no visitors admitted. It is about four miles west of the Los Angeles County-

Ventura County boundary on SR 126. The Native Daughters of the Golden West have placed a stone marker just inside the stone wall on the south side of the road.) The book is a romance about Ramona, the young heroine of mixed Indian and Scottish blood, adopted by a Spanish family, who elopes with Alessandro, a noble Indian. Alessandro is harassed by white homesteaders and meets a tragic end. The novel, romantic as it is, is a strong indictment of the cruelties Indians have suffered at the hands of white men and aroused public opinion in favor of better treatment of the Indians. The novel also gives a vivid picture of the old Spanish way of life in California, a way of life that was fast disappearing, if it was not already gone, when the book was written.

In 1887 Salvador Estudillo, the grandson of the original owner of the house, moved to Los Angeles and left the house in the hands of a caretaker. Legend has it that the caretaker exploited the house's tenuous connection with Helen Hunt Jackson and started a myth that the chapel in La Casa de Estudillo was the place where the originals of Ramona and Alessandro (the identity of the actual couple is not known) were married. The caretaker then proceeded to sell all the furnishings and even parts of the floor, roof, and windows to tourists who came to see where the most popular fictional heroine of her day had allegedly been married. When the caretaker ran out of things to sell, he disappeared, never to be heard from again. The house fell into disrepair until John D. Spreckles bought it in 1905 and financed its restoration in 1910. Thomas Getz, a showman, leased it from Spreckles and perpetuated the Ramona story. Further restoration was done in 1968–69, and the house now contains lovely period furnishings.

The *real* marriage place of Ramona, however, is the **Little Adobe Chapel** (a few blocks southeast along San Diego Avenue at 3961 Conde Street). Jackson never mentions the Estudillo house in *Ramona*, but she does describe this chapel. Father Antonio Ubach, the model for Father Gaspara in the novel, stated in an interview in the San Diego *Union* of June 25, 1905:

> Although it took place forty years ago, I remember it very well—how the couple came to me and asked me to marry them and how I was impressed with them. But it was not in the long adobe building which everybody points out as the place—that is the Estudillo place—but it took place in the little church which

stands not far away, near the old cemetery where the old mission bells are. Why, I would not marry them outside the church;
Catholics know that. Mrs. Jackson herself says that the wedding took place in the chapel, and I cannot imagine why any
other building is pointed out.

Old Town San Diego comprises a number of restored buildings, some of which are part of a state historic park (the Little
Adobe Chapel is not officially part of the historic park). In addition to La Casa de Estudillo, these include the **Seeley Stable,**
which displays horse-drawn vehicles and Western memorabilia;
the **San Diego** *Union* **Newspaper Building,** restored as a newspaper
office circa 1868, the year the paper was founded; and several
restored residences. The **Casa de Stewart,** constructed in the
1830s, was the home of John C. and Rosa Stewart. Mr. Stewart
was a shipmate of Richard Henry Dana. In the added final chapter
of *Two Years Before the Mast* Dana describes a visit he made to
the house in 1859. There are also several shops and restaurants in
the complex.

Old Globe Theatre. In Balboa Park.

The Old Globe Theatre was designed by Thomas Wood Stevens for the California Pacific International Exposition of 1935–
36. Stevens did a great deal of research in London, and the result
is probably the most authentic reproduction of the Elizabethan
theater in which Shakespeare's plays were first performed. The
National Shakespeare Festival performs Shakespearean plays in
the summer. During the rest of the year other plays are acted.
Inquire locally for schedules and prices.

San Francisco

San Francisco has a rich literary past—and present—but few
physical reminders of it. Many of the nineteenth-century buildings were destroyed in the 1906 earthquake and fire, and much of
what survived later fell victim to urban "progress." Most of the

sites where Mark Twain and other writers lived and worked are now occupied by skyscrapers in downtown San Francisco, and only the familiar street names remain.

The first significant appearance of San Francisco in American literature is in Richard Henry Dana's *Two Years Before the Mast,* which takes place at a time when California was still Mexican and San Francisco had just begun to develop an important port. Dana mentions **Mission Dolores** (Sixteenth and Dolores Streets), erected in 1776; it was around this mission, originally called Mission San Francisco de Asis, that the city began to grow.

The gold rush, of course, brought wealth and eventually culture to San Francisco, and made it the most exciting town in the West. In the early 1860s Mrs. Jessie Benton Frémont, wife of the Great Pathfinder, John C. Frémont, had a literary salon and encouraged Bret Harte in his writing. Harte had come to San Francisco around this time and worked as a typesetter for *The Golden Era,* a magazine that has been called the "cradle of California literature," and later began writing for it. He subsequently became the editor of *The Californian;* one of the people he hired to write for this publication was Mark Twain. In 1868 he became editor of *The Overland Monthly.* In this magazine appeared the works that made Harte world-famous: "The Luck of Roaring Camp" (1868), "The Outcasts of Poker Flat" (1869), and "Plain Language from Truthful James" (1870). In its early days, *The Overland Monthly* also published other California writers, among them Ina Coolbrith (the poet laureate of California), Charles Warren Stoddard, and Edward Rowland Sill.

Mark Twain arrived in town in 1864 after unsuccessful attempts at silver mining in Nevada and a successful attempt at writing in Virginia City, Nevada (which see), where he first used his pen name. He gives his impression of San Francisco in *Roughing It:*

> San Francisco, a truly fascinating city to live in, is stately and handsome at a fair distance, but close at hand one notes that the architecture is mostly old-fashioned, many streets are made up of decaying, smoke-grimed, wooden houses, and the barren sand-hills toward the outskirts obtrude themselves too prominently. Even the kindly climate is sometimes pleasanter when read about than personally experienced, for a lovely, cloudless

sky wears out its welcome by and by, and then when the longed
for rain does come it *stays*. Even the playful earthquake is
better contemplated at a dis—

However there are varying opinions about that.

Twain worked as a local reporter on the *Morning Call,* wrote
sketches for *The Golden Era* and *The Californian,* and was also a
correspondent for the *Territorial Enterprise* in Virginia City. It
was during his period in San Francisco that he made his three-
month trip to the Mother Lode country to try his luck at gold
mining, a trip that brought him not gold but material for "The
Celebrated Jumping Frog of Calaveras County" (see Calaveras
County).

Ambrose Bierce came to San Francisco after the Civil War.
He published a column called "Prattle" in Hearst's San Francisco *Examiner* and also wrote for *The Overland Monthly*. He
went to London in 1871 but returned in 1876 and served as the
editor of the San Francisco *Illustrated Wasp*. He was the virtual
literary dictator of San Francisco for twenty-five years. Other
members of the San Francisco literary circle included Joaquin
Miller (see Oakland), the muckraker Lincoln Steffens, Charles
Warren Stoddard, Ina Coolbrith, Edwin Markham (see San Jose),
and the naturalist John Muir (see Martinez).

A few vestiges from these early days remain. The **Bohemian
Club** (Post and Taylor Streets) is now an exclusive club, but at the
beginning it lived up to its name. Among its members were Mark
Twain, Bret Harte, Joaquin Miller, Ambrose Bierce, Edwin
Markham, and later Frank Norris (whose *McTeague* is set in a
less fashionable part of San Francisco), Jack London, and Gelett
Burgess, the humorist most famous for his nonsense verse "I
Never Saw a Purple Cow." Oscar Wilde dined here during his
American lecture tour in 1882 (but he liked Chinatown better). Set
in the façade of the Post Street side of the building is a bronze
bas-relief tablet by Jo Mora depicting characters from the stories
of Bret Harte. One of the sadder literary associations of the
Bohemian Club is that the poet George Sterling (see Carmel)
committed suicide in his room here in 1926.

The **Hearst Building** (Third and Market Streets) housed the
San Francisco *Examiner* when Bierce wrote for it. Gertrude

Atherton, Joaquin Miller, and Edwin Markham were also contributors at various times.

Russian Hill was the area where a number of writers lived in the nineteenth century. A row of cottages on Florence Street off Vallejo Street was home to several authors, including Gelett Burgess, who edited *The Lark,* a literary journal, while living here. **Ina Coolbrith Park** (corner of Taylor and Vallejo Streets) is on the site of the poet's home, which was destroyed in the 1906 earthquake. Coolbrith was very influential in the literary circles of her day and was the only female member of the Bohemian Club.

Two other writers are commemorated in this section of the city. **George Sterling Park** (Larkin and Greenwich Streets), reachable by a stairway from Hyde Street, is dedicated to the poet. **Bret Harte Terrace** is a small street off Francisco Street between Leavenworth and Jones.

Anthony Trollope visited San Francisco in 1875 and wrote with disdain that there was "a place called the Cliff House to which strangers are taken to hear seals bark." **Cliff House** still exists, although in greatly altered form, at Seal Rocks, overlooking the Pacific (where Great Highway and Geary Boulevard meet). It is now a bar and restaurant.

The most noteworthy literary landmark of San Francisco was, alas, torn down in 1959. This was the famous **"Montgomery Block,"** often affectionately called the "Monkey Block," at Montgomery and Washington Streets, where the Transamerica Pyramid now stands. Built in 1852, the Montgomery Block was an extraordinary building for its time. It was four stories high with an open courtyard in the middle and had three-foot-thick brick walls and Doric columns along the street level; it looked like a fortress. Inside it was sumptuous; the offices were large and there were a sun parlor, steam baths, and a billiard room. At first it was the most prestigious business address in the city. President Grant made business calls here, and so did Mark Twain and Bret Harte. Robert Louis Stevenson chartered the yacht *Casco* here for his voyage to the South Seas in 1888. Later, around the turn of the century, the Montgomery Block changed from a commercial to an artistic center, and the likes of Jack London, Ambrose Bierce, and George Sterling were associated with it. They especially enjoyed patronizing Duncan Nicol's Bank Exchange Saloon in the building, which was famous for its Pisco Punch. When Rudyard Kipling visited San Francisco he stepped into the Bank Exchange, by then a popular literary watering hole. But by the 1950s the Montgomery Block had fallen into disrepair, and it fell to the wrecker's ball in 1959. In 1969, after ten years as a parking lot, the site became the home of the controversial Transamerica Pyramid. The Bank Exchange Saloon has been resurrected in the lobby of the Pyramid. Some original items from the first saloon have been used and other paraphernalia have been faithfully recreated. On the walls, panels depict some of the famous characters who patronized the old Bank Exchange.

Robert Louis Stevenson was another writer who sojourned in San Francisco and left his mark. At the end of 1879 he came up from Monterey (which see) to be near his fiancée, Fanny Osbourne, who lived in Oakland. In a letter he describes his life here:

> Any time between eight and half-past nine in the morning, a slender gentleman in an ulster with a volume buttoned into the breast of it may be observed leaving 608 Bush Street and descending Powell with an active step. The gentleman is R.L.S.; the volume relates to Benjamin Franklin on whom he meditates one of his charming essays. He descends Powell, crosses Market, and descends in Sixth on a branch of the original Pine Street Coffee House . . . .

He then goes on to describe his breakfast, and how he spends the rest of his day. The boardinghouse on Bush Street where he stayed has been demolished, along with the rest of the places he mentions. He especially liked to sit on a bench in **Portsmouth Square** (at Kearny, Clay, and Washington Streets). Here there is a monument of Stevenson, a granite shaft surmounted by a galleon in full sail (the *Hispaniola* of *Treasure Island*), set in a grove of poplars. In the spring of 1880, Stevenson, always in frail health, became seriously ill, and was moved to the Oakland home of his fiancée, where he was cared for. He had recovered by May of that year and he and Fanny were married in San Francisco. They spent their honeymoon on Mount St. Helena (see Calistoga). As noted above, Stevenson returned to San Francisco in 1888, when he chartered the *Casco* and set sail for the South Pacific.

San Francisco, being the home of so many writers, has naturally served as the locale of a great many fictional works. It's impossible, of course, to mention them all, but here are a few. Jack London, who was born in San Francisco but grew up in Oakland (which see), has Humphrey Van Weyden in *The Sea Wolf* start off on his adventures from the **Hyde Street Pier** where he boards a ferry to Sausalito. The dentist's office in Frank Norris's *McTeague* is at Polk and California, in what is called **Polk Gulch.**

More recently, Dashiell Hammett immortalized many spots in San Francisco in his hard-boiled detective fiction. The private eye Sam Spade had his "offices" at **111 Sutter.** His Continental Op worked out of the **Flood Building** (Powell and Market), where Hammett himself actually worked when he was a Pinkerton man. The St. Mark Hotel in *The Maltese Falcon* is modeled on the **St. Francis** (Powell and Geary); this is where Sam Spade tailed Brigid O'Shaughnessy. Spade's partner Miles Archer was shot to death in an alley called **Burritt Street** at the Stockton Street tunnel. **John's Grill** (63 Ellis Street) is named in *The Maltese Falcon* and was frequented by Hammett; upstairs in the Maltese Falcon Room you can eat surrounded by photographs and memorabilia of the author and of the movie.

The **North Beach** section (not really a beach, it runs along Columbus Avenue south of Fisherman's Wharf and north of Chinatown) was the scene of the heyday of the Beat Generation of the 1950s. Its cafes were meeting places for Jack Kerouac, who depicted life here in *The Dharma Bums,* and the poets Gary Snyder, Kenneth Rexroth, Allen Ginsberg, and Lawrence Ferlinghetti. Ferlinghetti founded the **City Lights Bookstore,** which still flourishes at 261 Columbus Avenue. Here you can still browse among the paperbacks and the small literary magazines and find notices of poetry readings. Ferlinghetti published Allen Ginsberg's *Howl* and many other Beat poets.

A pleasant sidelight to a visit to San Francisco is a trip to **Muir Woods National Monument,** a wilderness area with a grove of redwoods dedicated to the writer and naturalist John Muir. It is in Marin County, twelve miles north of the Golden Gate Bridge via US 101 and SR 1.

For the full story of nineteenth-century literary San Francisco, see *San Francisco's Literary Frontier* by Franklin Walker.

The San Francisco *Examiner* has produced a lively booklet enti-
tled *A Booklover's Guide to San Francisco* (write to Examiner
Special Projects, the Hearst Building, Third and Market Streets,
San Francisco, CA 94103).

San Jose

Edwin Markham Home. 432 South Eighth Street. Open by appointment. Telephone 408-297-9141 or 293-2315. Free.

This three-story redwood building was the home of the poet
Edwin Markham (1852–1940) from 1857 to 1899. It was here that
he wrote his most famous poem, "The Man with the Hoe," inspired by a painting by Millet:

> Bowed by the weight of centuries he leans
> Upon his hoe and gazes on the ground,
> The emptiness of ages in his face,
> And on his back the burden of the world.
> Who made him dead to rapture and despair,
> A thing that grieves not and that never hopes,
> Stolid and stunned, a brother to the ox?
> Who loosened and let down this brutal jaw?
> Whose was the hand that slanted back this brow?
> Whose breath blew out the light within this brain? . . .

The poem was published in the San Francisco *Examiner* on
January 15, 1899. This plea for justice for the working man was
hugely successful. The popularity of the book *The Man with the
Hoe and Other Poems* later in 1899 enabled Markham to give up
teaching and devote his full time to writing.

COLORADO

One of the most interesting of early accounts of Colorado was written by an Englishwoman, Isabella Bird, who visited the Rockies in 1873 during a three-and-a-half-month Western trip. Bird, who later became the first female Fellow of the Royal Geographical Society, describes her adventures in *A Lady's Life in the Rocky Mountains,* recently reprinted. This intrepid woman wore Turkish trousers under her ankle-length skirt and climbed and rode horseback through the high mountains. She lived alone in a cabin near Lake Estes, helped neighboring pioneer women, had a sort of romance with a mysterious character called Mountain Jim, and made an ascent of Longs Peak (now part of Rocky Mountain National Park), which she described as "heaven-piercing, pure in its pearly luster, as glorious a mountain as the sun tinges red in either hemisphere. . . ." She deplored the settlers' hard life and the ugliness of the frontier towns but loved the majestic grandeur of the scenery.

Colorado has, of course, been the subject and setting for many Westerns, notably by William MacLeod Raine, Luke Short, and the omnipresent Zane Grey. And the romantic past of the mining boom has provided material for numerous popular novels about that era. Central City and Leadville, the most famous mining towns in Colorado, are now tourist attractions. Frank Waters, born in Colorado Springs, wrote a number of books about Colorado mining, including *Midas of the Rockies,* and a trilogy about the Pikes Peak region that begins with *The Wild Earth's Nobility.*

The state was a locale of one of Willa Cather's best novels: the first part of *The Song of the Lark* takes place in a Colorado town called Moonstone in the novel. She also used Mesa Verde (which see) as the scene for the story within a story of *The Professor's House*. Jean Stafford used her own youth in Colorado as the background for her novel *The Mountain Lion*.

Denver has been a lively newspaper town since the old mining days and produced one of the most famous newspapermen of his time, Gene Fowler (1890–1960), who was born there. He worked on the Denver *Post* in his youth, and his nonfiction book *Timberline* tells the story of the flamboyant men who ran that paper, Fred G. Bonfils and Harry Tammen. Several of his novels are set in Denver, also: *Trumpet in the Dust* and *Shoe the Wild Mare* in pioneer Denver and *Salute to Yesterday* in the modern city. Clyde Brion Davis also wrote for the *Post*. His best-known novel is *The Great American Novel* (1938), which has scenes in Denver. The oddball *Rocky Mountain Herald,* owned and edited by Thomas Hornsby Ferril and his wife Helen Ferril, began life in 1860 publishing nothing but legal notices and continued to publish them, plus stories and poems by eminent writers like Carl Sandburg and Bernard DeVoto. *The Rocky Mountain Herald Reader* is a selection of items from the paper.

Bent's Old Fort National Historic Site

8 miles northeast of La Junta on SR 194. Daily, May–Aug. 8–6, Sept.–Apr. 8–4. Free.

William Bent was the first permanent white settler in Colorado. In the early 1830s he and his brother, a fur trapper, built this trading post, which trappers used as a rendezvous point and to which Plains Indians came to trade. It was an important stopping place on the Santa Fe Trail, the principal overland route to the Southwest and Southern California before the railroad was built. Kit Carson, the legendary guide and frontiersman, was frequently employed by Bent's Fort; besides being the hero of scores of Westerns, he is the subject of Stanley Vestal's biography *Kit Carson*. John C. Frémont, who hired Carson as a guide, used Bent's Fort as a base from which he started on two of his expeditions (see California). Stanley Vestal's *'Dobe Walls* is a novel about the Santa Fe Trail that focuses on Bent's Fort, and David S. Lavender is the author of *Bent's Fort*. Harvey Fergusson's trilogy *Followers of the Sun* (1936) is an epic about the Santa Fe Trail.

Bent's Fort has been partially restored and there is a self-guided tour. Living history programs are presented in the summer.

Colorado Springs

Pioneers' Museum. 215 South Tejon. Daily except Mon., 10–5, Sun. 2–5. Free.

Helen Hunt (Jackson), a New Englander, took a trip to California in 1872, and because of ill health spent the winter of 1873–74 in Colorado Springs, which had become famous as a spa. A widow, she met William Sharpless Jackson, a banker and financier, and married him in 1875. Until her death in 1885 Colorado Springs was her home, although she traveled east and to California, where she did research for her famous novel *Ramona* (see San Diego and Hemet, California), which followed the publication of *A Century of Dishonor,* a report that indignantly chronicled the wrongs done to the American Indian by the United States Government. At her Colorado Springs home she wrote *Mercy Philbrick's Choice* (1876), a novel supposedly based on the life of her friend Emily Dickinson, much poetry, and two books with Colorado settings: *Bits of Travel at Home* and *Nelly's Silver Mine.*

When her house was demolished in the 1960s a portion of it was preserved for exhibit in the Pioneers' Museum, which has recently moved to this new location. The museum has an exhibit of Jackson mementos; the rebuilt part of Jackson's home, with original furnishings, will be on display on completion of the renovation of the museum's new home (inquire locally for latest information).

Helen Hunt Jackson died at the age of fifty-four and was buried under a cairn of stone near the summit of Cheyenne Mountain, at a spot called Inspiration Point. A trail leads up to the grave site from Seven Falls, but the author is no longer buried there. For several years after her death tourists came seeking relics. The vandalism got so bad that her widower had her body removed to Evergreen Cemetery in Colorado Springs.

Leadville

Leadville is most famous for the story of Horace A. W. Tabor and Baby Doe, the basis of the opera *The Ballad of Baby Doe* by Douglas Moore. Tabor struck it rich in 1878 and became Leadville's leading citizen. A year later he bought the famous Matchless, a fabulously rich silver mine. Meanwhile, Tabor's marriage to Augusta Tabor had begun to disintegrate. In 1881 Tabor deserted his wife and went to live with his mistress, Mrs. Elizabeth Doe. He married Baby Doe in 1883, and for ten years they lived in extravagant style, sometimes in a mansion in Denver and often traveling and staying in the finest hotels. The Silver Panic of 1893, however, left Tabor bankrupt. His dying words to Baby Doe, in 1899, were "Hold on to the Matchless." Baby Doe did just that, living in a cabin next to the mine for thirty-six years in abject poverty. In March 1935 she was found frozen to death in the cabin.

The **Matchless Mine** (2 miles east of town on East Seventh Street), along with Baby Doe's cabin, is open June–Labor Day, daily 9–5. A tour is given for a small fee.

The **Tabor Home,** at 116 East Fifth Street (open Memorial Day–Labor Day, daily 9–5:30, rest of year, daily except Sun. 9:30–5:30, closed Christmas, New Year's Day, Easter; small admission), is where Horace Tabor and his first wife Augusta lived until 1881, when they moved to Denver. (It was a short time later that Tabor left Augusta for Baby Doe.) It is a small, modest frame dwelling that has been restored with some original Tabor furnishings.

Most fascinating of all in Leadville is the **Tabor Opera House** at 308 Harrison Avenue (guided tours Memorial Day–Oct. 1, daily except Sat. 9–5:30, rest of year by appointment; telephone 303-486-1147). Built by Horace Tabor in 1879, when Leadville was at the peak of its mining prosperity, it is ornately decorated in Victorian style. The tour includes the backstage area and the dressing rooms, which have antique furniture, some of it original. Stars of the theater and opera performed here: the great actress Modjeska, Anna Held of the Ziegfeld Follies, and Houdini. The audience in the early days consisted mostly of rough miners, but they all had silver and gold to spend lavishly. Shows are now given here in summer.

Oscar Wilde appeared here on his American lecture tour in 1882. In his lecture "Impressions of America," delivered on his return to London, he called Leadville "the richest city in the world," and continued:

It has also got the reputation of being the roughest, and every man carries a revolver. I was told that if I went there they would be sure to shoot me or my travelling manager. I wrote and told them that nothing that they could do to my travelling manager would intimidate me. They are miners—men working in metals, so I lectured them on the Ethics of Art. I read them passages from the autobiography of Benvenuto Cellini and they seemed much delighted. I was reproved by my hearers for not having brought him with me. I explained that he had been dead for some little time which elicited the enquiry "Who shot him?" They afterwards took me to a dancing saloon where I saw the only rational method of art criticism I have ever come across. Over the piano was printed a notice:

PLEASE DO NOT SHOOT THE
PIANIST.
HE IS DOING HIS BEST.

The mortality among pianists in that place is marvellous. . . .

After Wilde's lecture to the miners the governor of the state took him to visit the Matchless Mine, where he was "shot down" in a bucket through the shaft for a banquet, which consisted of three courses, all of them whiskey. Wilde's large capacity for liquor impressed the miners, and they had him open a new silver lode, which they named the Oscar. They then presented the drill as a souvenir. In a letter he wrote:

> . . . I had hoped that in their simple, grand way they would have offered me shares in "The Oscar," but in their artless untutored fashion they did not. Only the silver drill remains as a memory of my night at Leadville.

A minor classic of sorts is *The Led-Horse Claim* (1883) by Mary Hallock Foote (1847–1938), who was the wife of a Leadville mining engineer. It was the first novel to use a Colorado boom town for its locale.

Other buildings of interest in Leadville are the Healy House–Dexter Cabin Museums, the House with the Eye, and the Heritage Museum and Gallery. The Chamber of Commerce, Box 861, Leadville, CO 80461, provides brochures and maps of Leadville and nearby historic mining areas.

Mesa Verde National Park

10 miles east of Cortez on US 160. Park open all year; Far View Visitor Center (16 miles south of entrance) open June–Labor Day, daily 8–5; museum at park headquarters (21 miles south of park entrance) open daily, June–Labor Day 8–6, rest of year to 5; free. Fee per vehicle for admission to park.

In 1915 Willa Cather journeyed again to the Southwest (she had been in Arizona in 1912), this time in the company of her friend Edith Lewis. On this trip she visited Mesa Verde for the first time. She had already seen cliff dwellings in Walnut Canyon, Arizona, and had used that place as the setting for a key episode in *The Song of the Lark,* completed just before she left on this Colorado trip. Now she wanted to see the more extensive dwellings at Mesa Verde.

Mesa Verde is a tableland some fifteen miles long and two thousand feet above the valley to the north. Honeycombed with canyons on the south side, it contains hundreds of ancient cliff dwellings in the huge caves and on the tops of the mesas. The Indians who inhabited these villages lived here for eight centuries, from around the sixth to the thirteenth centuries A.D., then abandoned their homes, for what reason precisely no one knows. During the latter half of the nineteenth century exploration by white men began, and some of the Mesa Verde was scientifically excavated. There were depredations by cowboys and others seeking artifacts to sell, however, and there was quite a struggle, both with mining interests and with the Ute tribe, before it was established as a national park in 1906 with the purpose of protecting these great ruins.

So when Cather visited Mesa Verde, it had been a national park for only a few years. The spectacular Cliff Palace, with 223 rooms, had only recently been excavated, the only access to the park was by horse and wagon, and there were as yet few visitors. Edith Lewis, in *Willa Cather Living,* writes of their visit here, and tells how they got lost in Soda Canyon when an inexperienced ranger accidentally led them astray; they had to wait hours until they were rescued. But the time was valuable for Cather, as Lewis recalls:

> The four or five hours that we spent waiting there were, I think, for Willa Cather the most rewarding of our whole trip to the Mesa Verde. . . . We were tired and rather thirsty, but not worried, for we knew we should eventually be found. We did not talk, but watched the long summer twilight come on, and the full moon rise up over the rim of the canyon. The place was very beautiful.

During this trip they met the brother of Richard Wetherill, one of the cowboys who had discovered Cliff Palace and Chapin Mesa. His story of how his brother came upon the intact village, and Cather's whole experience here, became the basis for the story within a story called "Tom Outland's Story" in her novel *The Professor's House,* published ten years later, in 1925. Tom and his friend Roddy Blake, both working as cowboys, come upon the "Blue Mesa," as she renamed Mesa Verde in the book, and discover its secret, the perfectly preserved abandoned Indian village sheltered under the rock:

> Far up above me, a thousand feet or so, set in a great cavern in the face of the cliff, I saw a little city of stone, asleep. It was as still as sculpture—and something like that. It all hung together, seemed to have a kind of composition: pale little houses of stone

nestling close to one another, perched on top of each other, with flat roofs, narrow windows, straight walls, and in the middle of the group a round tower.

It was beautifully proportioned, that tower, swelling out to a larger girth a little above the base, then growing slender again. There was something symmetrical and powerful about the swell of the masonry. . . . I knew at once that I had come upon a city of some extinct civilization, hidden away in this inaccessible mesa for centuries, preserved in the dry air and almost perpetual sunlight like a fly in amber, guarded by the cliffs and the river and the desert.

The two work all summer excavating. Tom realizes that these relics should be protected and goes to the Smithsonian Institution in Washington to try to persuade the government to take over the mesa and protect it, but he meets only with indifference. Frustrated, he returns to the mesa and discovers that Roddy has in the meantime sold the artifacts to a German archaeologist. He bitterly argues with his friend, but eventually accepts his share of the proceeds of the sale to use for a college education.

The park has a Ruins Road Drive on which self-guided tours can be taken. However, the cliff dwellings themselves can be entered only in the company of a ranger. Ranger-guided trips begin at the Visitor Center or museum and go to Spruce Tree House, Cliff Palace, Balcony House, and other sites. Camping is available in the park. Address inquiries to Superintendent, Mesa Verde National Park, CO 81330.

HAWAII

In May of 1843, twenty-four-year-old Herman Melville found himself in **Lahaina,** a whaling port at the western end of the island of Maui. The previous summer he had jumped ship from the whaler *Acushnet* in the Marquesas and had spent almost a month among tribesmen there, an experience that later was transformed into *Typee*. He got away from the Marquesas on another whaler that took him to Tahiti, where, in trouble again, he was put into the stockade. Finally, he signed on board still another whaling vessel that put him ashore at Lahaina. With little to do and still less money he left for Honolulu after about two weeks, where he found a job as a clerk and bookkeeper for a merchant. But in August 1843 Melville saw an opportunity to return to the United States by signing up as an ordinary seaman on a United States Navy warship that was anchored in the harbor of Honolulu. Melville did not much like Hawaii, and in an appendix to *Typee* gives an unflattering portrait of the corruption that the white man, including and perhaps especially the missionaries, brought to the Polynesian people of Hawaii.

Lahaina still has vestiges of its great days as a whaling center. (It makes an important appearance in James Michener's historical novel *Hawaii*.) The **Baldwin House** on Front Street (open daily 9:30–5; admission) is a restored medical missionary's house built in 1834. North along SR 30 in Kaanapali is **Whaler's Village,** an outdoor whaling museum and shopping complex with whale skeletons, scrimshaw, and other whaling relics on display among nineteenth-century-style shops. Off the coast is a whale migration route, but the goal of most people here is now to save the whale rather than to harpoon it.

Subsequent visits to the Hawaiian Islands by well-known writers were less haphazard than Melville's, and also more pleasant. Charles Warren Stoddard (1843–1909), a member of the San Francisco literary circle that included Mark Twain and Bret Harte, first visited Hawaii in 1864 and made several subsequent visits. His *South-Sea Idyls* (1873) is a series of sketches about his Hawaiian experiences.

In 1866 Mark Twain was sent to the Sandwich Islands (as they were then called) by the Sacramento *Union* to write travel reports. He describes his half-year sojourn there in detail in *Roughing It*. He was charmed by the beauty and exotic nature of the islands. Here is his first impression of Oahu:

> On a certain bright morning the Island hove in sight, lying low on the lonely sea, and everybody climbed to the upper deck to look. After two thousand miles of watery solitude the vision was a welcome one. As we approached, the imposing promontory of Diamond Head rose up out of the ocean, its rugged front softened by the hazy distance, and presently the details of the land began to make themselves manifest: first the line of beach; then the plumed cocoanut trees of the tropics; then cabins of the natives; then the white town of Honolulu, said to contain between twelve and fifteen thousand inhabitants spread over a dead level; with streets from twenty to thirty feet wide, solid and level as a floor, most of them straight as a line and few as crooked as a corkscrew.

While on Oahu he made excursions to Diamond Head and other spots on the island, and also interviewed survivors of a marine disaster who had been brought to Honolulu; this article was published in *Harper's Magazine*.

After his stay on Oahu Twain and some companions traveled to the island of Hawaii, the "big island." He visited **Kealakekua Bay** on the west coast, where Captain Cook was killed by natives in 1779.

> Near the shore we found "Cook's Monument"—only a cocoanut stump, four feet high and about a foot in diameter at the butt. It had lava boulders piled around its base to hold it up and keep it in its place, and it was entirely sheathed over, from top to bottom, with rough, discolored sheets of copper, such as

ships' bottoms are coppered with. Each sheet had a rude in-
scription scratched upon it—with a nail, apparently—and in
every case the execution was wretched. Most of these merely
recorded the visits of British naval commanders to the spot, but
one of them bore this legend:

> "Near this spot fell
> CAPTAIN JAMES COOK,
> The·Distinguished Circumnavigator, who Discovered these
> Islands A.D. 1778"

Now there is a **Captain Cook Memorial,** marked by a plaque and
accessible by boat or by trail along the bay.

Twain also writes about his visit to the City of Refuge, a
sacred sanctuary where criminals and taboo-breakers could find
safety and absolution. The remains of the temple can still be seen
at the **City of Refuge National Historical Park.** It is near the village
of Honaunau, a few miles south of Kealakekua Bay (Visitor
Center open daily 7:30–5:30). He also traveled to Kalauea Vol-
cano, which is now part of **Hawaii Volcanoes National Park.** He
passed through the town of **Waiohinu** (on SR 11 at the southern
end of the island). Here there is a tree known as **Mark Twain's
Monkeypod Tree.** Twain is said to have planted the tree, although
actually the original one was blown down in a storm in 1957 and
the one you see now is a new one growing from the roots of the
first one. On Maui, Twain, an inveterate sightseer, traveled
through the **Iao Valley,** with its mile-high gorge and famous Iao
Needle, a rock formation 1200 feet above the valley floor. Twain
called it the "Yosemite of the Pacific," and appropriately, it is
now a state park.

Robert Louis Stevenson arrived in **Honolulu** aboard his chartered yacht *Casco* in late January 1889 with his wife Fanny, his
stepson Lloyd Osbourne, and his mother, plus a cook, a maid,
and a captain and crew of four. The party had sailed from San
Francisco in June 1888 for the South Seas and had stopped at the
Marquesas and Tahiti. They left Tahiti on Christmas Day 1888,
sailing north to the Hawaiian Islands, but because of adverse
wind conditions it took them a whole month before they finally
arrived safely at Honolulu harbor. Fanny's daughter Belle had

been living in that city since 1882 with her artist husband Joseph Strong. Belle and her eight-year-old son Austin came out on a small boat to greet the Stevenson party.

Stevenson's health had improved during the ocean voyage and he was able to enjoy himself. He entertained Kalakaua, the last Hawaiian king, on the *Casco* two days after his arrival, and was impressed and amused by Kalakaua's enormous drinking capacity. The two became great friends, and Stevenson wrote much about him in his letters of this period. Stevenson released the *Casco* soon after and moved out to Waikiki, where he could be away from the social life of Honolulu, which did not interest him much, and where he could have the isolation he needed to write. The family rented a rambling Hawaiian-style house on the beach. He used a shack away from the main house to work in, and it was there that he finished *The Master of Ballantrae* and began work on *The Wrong Box*. The Banyan Court of the **Moana Hotel** (2365 Kalakaua Avenue) on the beachfront contains a century-old banyan known as the **Robert Louis Stevenson tree,** under which RLS reputedly sat and talked to the thirteen-year-old Princess Kaiulani, the half-Hawaiian daughter of his friend A. S. Cleghorn, a fellow Scot who was a successful Honolulu merchant and had married the sister of King Kalakaua.

Stevenson made a brief visit to the island of Hawaii, to the Kona coast, a trip that provided him with material for his short story "The Bottle Imp." On his way he was allowed to visit the leper colony at Kalaupapa on Molokai. Father Damien had died just a month before, and Stevenson much regretted not having been able to meet the man who had founded the colony. Later, when he was in Sydney, Australia, Stevenson read a letter in a newspaper by Reverend Charles M. Hyde attacking Father Damien. Stevenson wrote a scathing reply, defending the priest and attacking Hyde, and condemning the attitudes of some *haoles* (Caucasians) toward the native Hawaiian population.

By spring of 1889 Stevenson had decided to leave Hawaii. He felt "oppressed with civilization" and also found the climate not warm enough for him(!). He and Fanny chartered another boat and on June 24, 1889, set sail again. They eventually settled in Samoa, where he died in 1894. Stevenson did, however, make another trip to Oahu in 1893, when he stayed at a hotel again at

Waikiki and visited Queen Liliuokalani, who had recently been deposed. On the grounds of the **Waioli Tea Room** (3016 Oahu Avenue), a few minutes inland from Waikiki, is the "little grass shack" where he also stayed briefly in 1893 as the guest of Princess Kaiulani. Some of the stories in *Island Nights' Entertainments* (1893) have Hawaiian backgrounds, and travel sketches in *The Eight Islands* (1896) deal with Hawaii and the South Seas.

The peripatetic Joaquin Miller showed up in the islands at the end of 1894 as a correspondent for *The Overland Monthly* and several other newspapers. He wrote eyewitness accounts of the fighting that was going on during the short-lived royalist counter-revolution after the deposition of Queen Liliuokalani. He was discovered in the Manoa Valley wearing his characteristic sombrero and leather leggings and was brought back to Honolulu, where he was identified as the famous author. Edward Joesting, in *Hawaii: An Uncommon History* (1972), recounts that Miller was a guest at the home of President and Mrs. Dole, but that when it was learned that Miller was living with a pregnant Mexican girl in a Honolulu hotel, the poet was advised to leave the islands, which he did quite quickly.

Another great literary traveler, adventurer, and sailor, Jack London, sailed with his wife Charmian to the South Pacific in 1907 aboard the *Snark*. They anchored in Pearl Harbor in May 1907 after a twenty-seven-day voyage from San Francisco. While waiting for the engine of the boat to be repaired they stayed in a cottage at Pearl Harbor. They also spent some time as the guests of Lorrin Thurston in Honolulu and surfed at Waikiki. London went to Maui and stayed with the Louis von Tempsky family at their ranch at Haleakala. Edward Joesting tells of their excursions on the slopes and in the crater of Haleakala, now a national park with a visitor center, observation point, and guided tours of the crater. Jack and Charmian returned to Hawaii in March 1915 for a three-month stay and led an active social life. They returned once more at the end of 1915 and remained until July of the following year, when they left to attend a gathering of the Bohemian Club at Pacific Grove on the Monterey Peninsula in California. By that time, he was a very sick man, and although he had planned to come back to Hawaii, he never did; he died in November 1916. London set a number of his stories in the islands. "Koolau, the Leper," for instance, takes place in the inaccessible **Kalalau Valley** on **Kauai.** The valley can be viewed from **Kalalau Lookout,** which can be reached from Kekaha by driving to the end of SR 55. London's book *The Cruise of the Snark* is an account of his South Seas voyage. Charmian wrote *Our Hawaii* (1917), a book of reminiscences, after her husband's death.

Many other authors visited Hawaii and wrote about it. Rupert Brooke came for a season in 1913 during a trip to the Pacific islands and wrote a poem calld "Waikiki." Somerset Maugham made a stopover in Honolulu in 1916 on one of his voyages to the tropics and wrote a story called "Honolulu." One of J. P. Marquand's finest short stories is "Lunch at Honolulu," included in *Thirty Years* (1954). He lived in that city in the 1930s, when he began writing the "Mr. Moto" stories, and served as a naval attaché there in World War II. The poet Genevieve Taggard (1894–1948) spent part of her girlhood in Hawaii as the daughter of a missionary. *Hawaiian Hilltop* (1923) and *Origin: Hawaii* (1947) are two of her books. *A Hawaiian Reader* (1959), edited by A. Grove Day and Carl Stroven, is a collection of writing about Hawaii by authors of the nineteenth and twentieth centuries. Incidentally, Waikiki is the setting for one of the most famous works of subliterature: the Halekulani Hotel, at 2199 Kalia Road at the end of Lewers Street, is where *The House Without a Key,* the first Charlie Chan novel, by Earl Derr Biggers, takes place.

One of the finest novels about World War II is, of course, *From Here to Eternity* (1951) by James Jones. Its action takes place on **Oahu,** at Schofield Barracks and Pearl Harbor just prior to the Japanese attack. (Some of the film version was shot on location at Schofield Barracks, which is inland near Wahiawa.) More recently, N. Richard Nash's novel *East Wind, Rain* (1977) also deals with the naval base at Pearl Harbor before the attack, and its climactic scene is the bombing. A navy boat provides free tours of **Pearl Harbor** and the **U.S.S.** *Arizona* **National Memorial,** which floats above the sunken hull of the *Arizona.* During the attack on December 7, 1941, 1177 men were killed on the *Arizona* alone, and more than a thousand of them still lie buried here under the water. To reach the memorial from Honolulu take SR 90 (Kamehameha Highway) west and exit at Halawa Gate.

Finally, many would consider James Michener's sweeping historical novel *Hawaii* indispensable reading for a trip to the islands. His fictionalized account of Hawaii traces its history from its volcanic origins and early Polynesian migrations through modern times.

IDAHO

The journals of Lewis and Clark record their passage through Idaho. The **Lewis and Clark Highway** (US 12) is a scenic road that parallels the path of the 1805 expedition. The **Lolo Trail,** the actual—and rough—route, can be reached via a Forest Service Road north of US 12 at the Powell ranger station (west of Lolo Pass, near Montana border). Canoe Camp in Clearwater National Forest is where the expedition built dugout canoes and started the final leg of their voyage down the Snake and ultimately to the mouth of the Columbia River (see Fort Clatsop, Astoria, Oregon). Lewiston, Idaho, and adjoining Clarkston, Washington, are named in honor of the explorers. Washington Irving's *Adventures of Captain Bonneville* is a narrative of a somewhat later explorer who traveled through the northwest in the early 1830s; the Idaho portion of his journey went from the Salmon River south to the Snake.

At **Spalding,** in **Nez Perce National Historical Park,** is the site of the **Spalding Mission,** where Eliza and Henry Spalding set up their headquarters after moving from their first mission at Lapwai. The Spaldings, friends and colleagues of Marcus and Narcissa Whitman (see Walla Walla, Washington), are buried here, near a museum that includes exhibits about them. Their original mission at **Lapwai** is two miles south of Spalding, at Thunder Hill.

Certainly the most prominent of Idaho writers was Vardis Fisher (1895–1968), who was born in Annis, Idaho. His early novels, *Toilers of the Hills* (1928) and *Dark Bridwell* (1931), both have Idaho settings, the first on a farm in eastern Idaho, the second on the Snake River. He is best known for his tetralogy of autobiographical novels about the life of Vridar Hunter and his quest for the meaning of life; all four novels—*In Tragic Life*

(1932), *Passions Spin the Past* (1934), *We Are Betrayed* (1935), and *No Villain Need Be* (1936)—have a locale in the southeastern section of the state. Fisher is also known for his epic novel about the early Mormons, *Children of God* (see Utah) and for his ambitious series of novels about the development of man called *Testament of Man*.

Hailey

Blaine County Historical Museum. North Main Street. June 15–Sept. 15, Wed.–Mon. 10–5. Small admission.

Ezra Pound was born in Hailey in 1885, when it was a frontier mining town. There had been silver strikes in the area and Pound's father had come to Hailey to run the U.S. Land Office. But the family moved back east when Ezra was less than two years old, first to New York, and shortly thereafter to Philadelphia, where the poet grew up. Nothing of Idaho comes through in Pound's poetry, but his place of birth nevertheless remembers him. The Blaine County Historical Museum has among its exhibits a small collection of Pound items, including books, photographs, and newspapers clippings. The house where he was born, still privately owned, is a two-story frame house on Second Street South. It was built by Pound's father.

The town of Hailey was named for John Hailey (1835–1921), who wrote the first complete history of the state of Idaho. Hailey is a short distance south of Ketchum and Sun Valley.

Ketchum

Ketchum is one mile southwest of the resort of Sun Valley, in the Sawtooth Mountains. Ernest Hemingway was attracted to the area by its opportunities for hunting and the outdoor life. He first came to Sun Valley in late 1939 and wrote some of *For Whom the*

Bell Tolls, "the part with all the snow in it," as he later wrote, in Suite 206 of the **Sun Valley Lodge,** which at the time was only a few years old. He returned frequently, usually staying in rented homes in Ketchum. In 1959 he bought a house in the Warm Springs area of Ketchum. It is still owned by his widow, Mary Welsh Hemingway, and is not open to visitors. Mrs. Hemingway writes movingly of Hemingway's last years here in her autobiography, *How It Was* (1976). It was in his Ketchum home that Hemingway committed suicide with a shotgun on July 2, 1961. He is buried in the Ketchum cemetery at the north edge of the town on US 93. A **memorial bust** of him is on Trail Creek Road, a half mile north of Sun Valley.

ILLINOIS

The literature of Illinois represents both ends of the spectrum of American writing. From the Chicago of the late nineteenth century up to the present time has come writing that epitomized the excitement and turbulence of American urban life, while other Illinois authors, like Edgar Lee Masters, have explored the life of small-town America. And Abraham Lincoln has become an almost iconographic figure, the central character in works of fiction, drama, and poetry as well as the subject of biographies and histories; Robert E. Sherwood's Pulitzer Prize-winning play *Abe Lincoln in Illinois* is perhaps the most familiar. (Lincoln sites are numerous in the state, but are not covered in this volume. A map of Lincoln sites in Illinois, Indiana, and Kentucky is available from Illinois Lincoln Heritage Trail Council, 702 West Bloomington, Champaign, IL 61820, or from the Springfield Convention and Tourism Commission, C-15, INB Center, Springfield, IL 62701.) Lincoln is, of course, also the subject of a monumental biography by Illinois author Carl Sandburg (see Galesburg). Gwendolyn Brooks, who grew up in Chicago, is now poet laureate of Illinois, an honor formerly held by Sandburg.

An important early Illinois writer was James Hall (1793–1868), who traveled around the territory as a circuit judge. He became an editor in frontier Illinois, working on the *Illinois Gazette* and the *Illinois Intelligencer* and founding the *Illinois Monthly Magazine,* the first literary periodical west of Ohio, in 1830. He was very prolific, producing in his stories, sketches, and essays a fine record of pioneer life and the legends of the frontier. Among his published works are *Letters from the West* (1828), *Legends of the West* (1832), and *Sketches of History, Life, and Manners in the West* (1834).

An interesting view of the pastoral Illinois of the mid-nineteenth century is *Summer on the Lakes* (1844) by Margaret Fuller, the brilliant New Englander who was an associate of Emerson and editor of *The Dial*.

Chicago

Carl Sandburg's famous poem "Chicago" was published in 1914 in *Poetry: A Magazine of Verse*, which had been founded in Chicago in 1912 by Harriet Monroe. (The poem was included in Sandburg's *Chicago Poems*, published in 1916). Sandburg, and *Poetry*, were part of the "Chicago Renaissance" that lasted from the years just before World War I to the early 1920s, and that also included such figures as Vachel Lindsay, Hamlin Garland, Floyd Dell, Theodore Dreiser, Edgar Lee Masters, Sherwood Anderson, and Ben Hecht.

Chicago literature has been closely tied to journalism. One of the earliest Chicago writers, the poet Eugene Field (see St. Louis), wrote a column for the Chicago *Daily News*. And Henry B. Fuller, the author of the novel *The Cliff Dwellers* (1893), set in a Chicago apartment house and one of the first successful novels about American big-city life, was a book reviewer for various Chicago newspapers; he was also active in the publication of *Poetry*. The humorist Finley Peter Dunne wrote his famous "Mr. Dooley" essays for the Chicago *Evening Post* beginning in the 1890s. Sandburg's years in Chicago, through the early 1930s, were spent as a newspaper reporter and correspondent, mainly for the *Daily News*. Theodore Dreiser also worked as a newspaperman in Chicago for a time. His autobiographical novel *Dawn* describes his life there; *Sister Carrie* (in part) and *The Titan* are also set in Chicago. Ring Lardner wrote a popular column in the Chicago *Tribune* and tells of his life as a Chicago newspaperman in *The Big Town*. Ben Hecht was perhaps the epitome of Chicago newspapermen. His novel *Erik Dorn* is based on his experiences as a correspondent for the *Daily News*, and his play *The Front Page*, written with Charles MacArthur, hilariously depicts the frantic, crazy pace of life as a big-city reporter. Hecht describes in his autobiography *A Child of the Century* how he haunted saloons, slums, theaters, police stations, jails, and scenes of crimes as a young Chicago reporter.

The Chicago novel has always been in the realistic mode, and many of the important ones are examples of that intensified realism called naturalism, in which social and economic factors take precedence over individual characters. Henry B. Fuller's *The Cliff Dwellers,* already mentioned, was one of the first American novels of this type. Frank Norris's *The Pit* (1903) is about speculation in wheat on the Chicago Board of Trade, and Upton Sinclair's muckraking *The Jungle* (1906) is a grim and brutal portrait of the workings of the Chicago stockyards. Dreiser's fiction, too, is of course in this mode. James T. Farrell, born and raised in Chicago, carried on this naturalistic tradition in the 1930s with his famous *Studs Lonigan* trilogy, about a tough Irish kid from the South Side of Chicago. His five Danny O'Neill novels are also about the Irish of Chicago. Richard Wright, who lived in the black slums of Chicago during the Depression, provided a harrowing picture of what it was like to be poor and black in the big city in his masterpiece *Native Son* (1940). Nelson Algren also depicted the seamy side of Chicago life in such novels as *The Man with the Golden Arm,* set in the slums of the West Side, and *A Walk on the Wild Side.*

The most famous writer of today's Chicago is Saul Bellow. Augie March, from the Northwest Side, had his adventures here, and Charles Citrine tries to cope in *Humboldt's Gift.*

The richness of Chicago literature is unfortunately not matched by a richness of literary sites. The places associated with these works have either been torn down, were and still are in deteriorating neighborhoods, or have gone downhill since the time the books were written. Chicago is a city of many fine art and science museums, but like many other large cities, it has not been able to preserve many relics of its literary past, although a few remain. The **Fine Arts Building** (410 South Michigan Avenue) was where *The Little Review,* edited by Margaret Anderson, had its first offices in 1914 and where the Little Theatre, run by Maurice and Nellie Browne, operated from 1912 to 1917, during the Chicago Renaissance. The **Chicago *Tribune* Tower** (435 North

Michigan Avenue), a Gothic-style skyscraper, offers free tours of its editorial department and printing plant (reservations required; write Plant Tours, Chicago Tribune, zip 60611, or phone 312-222-3993). The **Chicago Public Library Cultural Center** (78 East Washington Street at Michigan Avenue) has recently been renovated (but not without some controversy; many Chicagoans were unhappy about the loss of this building as the functioning main library). A landmark building in Beaux Arts style erected at the turn of the century, it has Tiffany-designed mosaics, two stained-glass domes which have been backlighted, walls and staircases of Carrara marble, and murals with inscriptions in various languages in praise of literature. Check locally for schedule and special exhibits.

One place worth a visit is **Hull House** (800 South Halsted on the campus of the University of Illinois at Chicago Circle; Mon.–Fri. 10–4, Sun. 1–5; closed holidays; free), the restored mansion where Jane Addams started her famous settlement house in 1889. Addams's *Twenty Years at Hull House* (1910) is something of a classic in autobiographical writing.

Oak Park, a suburb west of Chicago, has a literary distinction of its own. This upper-middle-class community, which has numerous homes designed by Frank Lloyd Wright around the turn of the century, was where Ernest Hemingway was born and grew up. His birth took place in 1899 in the house at **339** (originally 439) **North Oak Park Avenue.** In 1905 his parents rented a house north of the Oak Park Library, but shortly after, in 1906, the family moved to a large new house at **600 North Kenilworth Avenue,** where Ernest grew up. (These homes are not open to the public, but of course may be viewed from the outside.) His father was a doctor, and he spent a reasonably happy and secure childhood here, going to the local grammar school and to Oak Park–River Forest Township High School, where he wrote for the school's literary magazine and its newspaper, and from which he was graduated in 1917. The Historical Society of Oak Park and River Forest, located in the **Farson-Mills House** at Pleasant Street and Home Avenue (tours conducted free on Sundays, 1–3 p.m.), has Hemingway memorabilia on display, along with Frank Lloyd Wright items. (The **Frank Lloyd Wright Home and Studio** at Chicago and Forest Avenues has guided tours for the public.)

Another literary figure who lived in Oak Park was Edgar Rice Burroughs, the creator of Tarzan, who made his home at **414 August Boulevard** during the 1910s. For information on tours of Oak Park write Chamber of Commerce, 948 Lake Street, Oak Park, IL 60301.

In July 1978 the first **Oak Park Festival** was held. This featured several different tours highlighting the architectural and cultural treasures of the community; one of these tours was a literary one to Hemingway's and Burroughs's homes, and to the stamping grounds of other literary figures like Carl Sandburg, Charles MacArthur, Vincent Starrett, and Kenneth Fearing. Write the Chamber of Commerce or Oak Park Festival, 655 Lake Street, Oak Park, IL 60301, for details on possible future events.

Galesburg

Carl Sandburg Birthplace. 331 East Third Street. Daily, Tues.–Sat. 9–12, 1–5, Sun. 1–5; closed Thanksgiving, Christmas, New Year's Day. Free.

Carl Sandburg was born in this small workingman's shack on January 6, 1878, to Clara and August Sandburg, who were Swedish immigrants. His unlettered father worked as a blacksmith in the nearby yards of the Chicago, Burlington & Quincy Railroad. In his memoirs of his early years, *Always the Young Stranger,* Sandburg wrote:

> Of the house where I was born I remember nothing. I sucked at my mother's breasts there, had hundreds of changes of diapers and took healthy spankings there yet memory is a blank on those routine affairs. My sister Mary once pointed at the cradle in later years and said, "When they took me out they put him in." And a year and a half later they took me out to put Mart in. The cradle stood on three legs at each end, and mother told Mary that father made the cradle with his own hands. Mary said too that before I was three I ran away from home one afternoon and mother sent her to the C.B. & Q. shops and she brought father home from the shop and he found me a few blocks away going nowhere in particular.

The family moved to another house in 1879 and lived in various houses in Galesburg. Carl left school after the eighth grade and had a succession of jobs in Illinois and on the road in Kansas City, Denver, and Omaha, including ones as milkman, porter in a barbershop, and dishwasher. He came back to Galesburg in 1898 to be an apprentice house painter but soon enlisted and served briefly in Puerto Rico during the Spanish-American War. Coming back to Galesburg, he enrolled in Lombard College, where he edited the college newspaper. But in 1902, with only a few months to go before graduating, he left Lombard, took more odd jobs (like selling stereopticon equipment door to door), and wandered all over the country. In 1904 he once again returned to Galesburg, where Professor Philip Green Wright, his favorite teacher at Lombard, published Sandburg's first collection of verse, *In Reckless Ecstasy,* and two other books of his poetry at his tiny Asgard Press. In 1906 Sandburg left Galesburg for good and went to Chicago, where he stayed briefly (he returned, of course, for a much longer stay, in 1912), and then went to Wisconsin, where he met and married Lillian ("Paula," as he called her) Steichen.

Galesburg itself was a kind of epitome of the prairie town of the nineteenth century. In addition to Lombard College it had Knox College (still operating, at Cherry and South Streets), founded in 1837 and site of one of the Lincoln-Douglas debates—Sandburg, the biographer of Lincoln, grew up with a piece of Lincoln history at his doorstep. Sandburg wrote in *Always the Young Stranger* of Galesburg's typical pioneer immigrant mix of Yankees, Swedes, Scotch-Irish from Kentucky, Irish, and Germans:

> This small town of Galesburg, as I look back at it, was a piece of the American Republic. Breeds and blood strains that figure in history were there for me, as a boy, to see and hear in their faces and their ways of talking and acting.

The Carl Sandburg Birthplace was dedicated in 1946 after Sandburg's sister Mary helped identify the house as the authentic birthplace. Through the efforts of the Carl Sandburg Birthplace Association it was restored. The furnishings now on display are very simple and utilitarian, typical of a poor workingman's home of the day. A few of the pieces, including the kitchen table and three living room chairs, were used by the Sandburg family, and there are also photographs of Sandburg's parents and the family Bible.

In 1949 the addition on the rear of the house, which had been built years before by a carpenter who occupied the house, was refurbished as a museum of Sandburg memorabilia and named the Lincoln Room. The focus is on Lincoln and Sandburg's great biography, but other Sandburg items are also displayed, among them rare editions of his poetry published in Galesburg by the Asgard Press, a complete collection of books autographed by him that he had presented to Alfred Harcourt, his publisher, and the typewriter on which the author wrote *The Prairie Years* and *Rootabaga Stories*. Over the mantel hangs a portrait of Lincoln painted by N. C. Wyeth.

A park has been landscaped behind the house. In the center is a large boulder called Remembrance Rock, after Sandburg's only novel, of the same name. In *Remembrance Rock* Sandburg writes of a man who comes upon a boulder that seems to embody elements of history in it: "Also he had told others he named the boulder Remembrance Rock, for it should be a place to come and remember." After the poet's death in 1967 his ashes were buried beneath the rock, according to his request, so that the boulder now serves as a memorial to Sandburg himself.

Petersburg

Edgar Lee Masters Memorial Museum. Eighth and Jackson Streets. May 15–Labor Day, daily except Mon., 1–5. Free.

Edgar Lee Masters (1868–1950), author of *Spoon River Anthology* (1915), lived in this modest wooden house during his early boyhood. He was born in Garnett, Kansas, but his family soon moved to Petersburg. Masters wrote in his autobiography *Across Spoon River* (1936) that "altogether I was not happy in this house" and says that he much preferred his grandparents' farm, where he found a warmth missing from his parents' home.

The house has been restored and furnished in the style of the 1870s, when Masters lived here, and also contains the desk he worked at while he was living in New York City, at the Chelsea Hotel, later in life. Scrapbooks containing items about Masters and other family memorabilia are also on display.

When he was eleven years old, the Masters family moved to **Lewistown,** Illinois, northwest of Petersburg across the Illinois River, in the Spoon River country. The boyhood home of Masters in Lewistown still stands at the southeast corner of Main and C Streets. This is where he lived from 1883 to 1891 (it is now an insurance agency office and is not open to the public). Lewistown has a number of other historic sites. For information write Lewistown Society for Historic Preservation, Lewistown, IL 61542.

It was these two towns that later provided him with the prototypes of the characters who speak from their graves in his famous collection of poems. He wrote in the magazine *The American Mercury:*

> The names I drew from both the Spoon River and the Sangamon River neighborhoods, combining first names here with surnames there, and taking some also from the constitutions and State papers of Illinois.

Spoon River Anthology is a landmark in American literature and created a sensation, when it was first published, for its naturalism and honest exposure of the life of a small community. Many of the local people he based his characters on are buried in **Oak Hill Cemetery** in Lewistown (a few blocks north of the square on Main Street) and in **Oakland Cemetery** in Petersburg (on Oakland Avenue), where they "all, all, are sleeping on the hill." Like other writers from small midwestern towns—Sherwood Anderson and Sinclair Lewis come readily to mind—Masters exposed the underside of small-town life, its scandals, corruption, pettiness, and unhappiness, and like other writers too, he was resented by the hometown folks who thought they had been betrayed. But he is honored now in Petersburg (the city owns the Memorial) and is buried in Oakland Cemetery, among those he wrote about.

Also buried here is Ann Rutledge, supposed to have been Abraham Lincoln's first love, whose "epitaph" is in *Spoon River*

Anthology. New Salem, where Lincoln lived from 1831 to 1837, was just two miles south of Petersburg, and in fact, Lincoln surveyed the site for the town of Petersburg. New Salem has been restored as **Lincoln's New Salem State Park,** a re-creation of the town as Lincoln knew it. It was here that he met Anne Rutledge, and Rutledge Tavern is part of that restoration. Anne Rutledge was reinterred in Oakland Cemetery and lines from Masters's poem about her were carved on her headstone.

For information about the Spoon River Valley Scenic Drive write Box 58, Ellisville, IL 61431.

Springfield

Vachel Lindsay Home. 603 South Fifth Street. 1-hour tour. June 1–Sept. 1, 9–5. Nominal admission.

In this city of Lincoln, with the Lincoln Home National Historic Site, Lincoln's tomb, and many other Lincoln sites, Vachel Lindsay is Springfield's second celebrity. Unlike his Illinois contemporary Carl Sandburg, who was born into poverty, Vachel Lindsay had a happy and secure childhood. Born in 1879, the son of a doctor, he lived in this comfortable, substantial home all his life. After attending high school in Springfield, he went to Hiram College in Ohio for a few years, and then studied art, first in Chicago and then in New York, but he always returned home to Illinois. He made several extensive walking tours in his youth. In 1908 he traveled through the South, in 1910 from New York to Ohio; and in 1912 he made his famous walking trip from Illinois to New Mexico, trading his collection of poems *Rhymes to Be Traded for Bread* for his meals. In the years immediately following he published some of his best-known poems, "General Booth Enters into Heaven" and "The Congo." The spirit of Lincoln found its way into many of his works, particularly his writings about Springfield: "Abraham Lincoln Walks at Midnight" is one of the more widely read of his poems, and in "On the Building of Springfield" he says, "We must have many Lincoln-hearted men."

Lindsay was a popular public speaker and recited his poems frequently on the lecture circuit. His poetry was, in fact, written to be read aloud, and he was famous for his theatrical delivery. He was imbued with a crusading spirit, part of which involved the desire to make poetry popular with the masses. In the last few years of his life he found himself troubled by artistic conflicts and financial struggles. He committed suicide in 1931.

His home is now open to the public as a museum. Much of it has been preserved intact as Vachel Lindsay knew it, with beautiful wood doors and stairway, huge windows, and good furniture. There are also drawings and paintings by Lindsay hanging on the walls and a large collection of books by and about the poet. In the library the visitor can hear recordings of Lindsay reciting his poems just as he did in front of audiences years ago; the chanting rhythms and the dramatic intonations are quite impressive.

INDIANA

The first Indiana writer of importance was Edward Eggleston (1837–1902), who wrote realistic novels about frontier Indiana. Born in the village of Vevay on the Ohio River, he became a Methodist minister. His *The Hoosier Schoolmaster* (1871), about a teacher in the days before the Civil War, became one of the most widely read books of its day and one of the earliest regional novels in American literature. Eggleston published a sequel, *The Hoosier Schoolboy,* in 1883. He also wrote several other interesting novels, including *The Circuit Rider* (1874), which concerns the impact of Methodism on the newly settled middle western frontier and which was based on his own experiences; *Roxy* (1878), about a young girl in frontier Indiana; and *The Graysons* (1887), one of the earliest works of fiction to include Lincoln (in this case as a young Indiana lawyer) as a character. The archetypal American country world of cornhuskings, barn-raisings, square dances, quilting bees, and camp meetings is vividly depicted in Eggleston's work. A good place to get the flavor of pioneer Indiana is at the **Conner Prairie Pioneer Settlement** (18 miles northeast of Indianapolis via I-465, in Noblesville; early Apr.–early Nov., Tues.–Sat. 9:30–5, Sun. 10:30–5; admission), a model pioneer community with twenty-five buildings, including a blacksmith shop and a pottery workshop, plus craft demonstrations.

That world also appeared in the writings of the Indiana poet James Whitcomb Riley (1849–1916), whose popularity in his time was enormous. (See Greenfield and Indianapolis.)

A generation later, Booth Tarkington (1869–1946), born in Indianapolis, affectionately but astutely explored middle-class, small-town America in books like *Penrod, Seventeen,* and *Alice*

Adams (winner of the 1922 Pulitzer Prize). Tarkington served in the Indiana legislature in 1902–03, and his first novel, *The Gentleman from Indiana* (1899), about a crusading young newspaper editor who fights political corruption and is elected to congress, reflects his early interest in politics. His serious novel, *The Magnificent Ambersons,* which won the Pulitzer Prize in 1919, is a study of the decline of a kind of American aristocracy in a midwestern town as it is replaced by an industrial aristocracy.

A famous Indiana novel is *Raintree County* (1948) by Ross Lockridge, Jr., a long Civil War epic tracing the history of an Indiana community called Waycross. Jessamyn West's *Friendly Persuasion* also takes place during the Civil War; it is a story of Quakers living on a southern Indiana farm.

Bloomington

Lilly Library. East Seventh Street at Fine Arts Plaza, Indiana University campus. Mon.–Fri. 9–4, Sat. 9–12, 2–5, Sun. 2–5. Tours by appointment (telephone 812-337-2452).

The Lilly Library at Indiana University has one of the finest collections of rare books (about 100,000) and manuscripts (over a million) in the country. It numbers in its possessions medieval manuscripts, examples of early printing, including the New Testament portion of a Gutenberg Bible, and historical documents relating to the discovery and exploration of the New World and to early American history. A special collection of works by Indiana authors includes letters and manuscripts of James Whitcomb Riley and the autograph manuscript of Lew Wallace's *Ben-Hur*.

Brook

George Ade's Hazelden Home. 2½ miles east of Brook on SR 16. Open only for social affairs and group tours. Contact George Ade Memorial Association, Brook, IN 47922.

George Ade (1866–1944), one of America's greatest humorists, was born in Kentland, Indiana, about fifteen miles southwest of Brook. He first gained fame for his "Artie" stories in the Chicago *Record* in the 1890s. His most enduring book is *Fables in Slang* (1899), a collection of humorous stories and sketches, written not really in slang but in an exaggeratedly ornate colloquial prose, about ordinary people and the triumph of common sense. He was also an extremely successful playwright. *The County Chairman* (1903) was a funny play about political corruption, and *The College Widow* was a hit comedy of 1904.

Ade took up residence at Hazelden Farm in 1915 and lived there until his death. The English-style manor house fell into disrepair after Ade died (he never married, and so had no wife or children to leave it to), but the George Ade Memorial Association finally was formed to restore the house. There's not enough traffic to open the house to individual visitors, but it is rented regularly for parties, weddings, and other social events, and groups can arrange in advance for a tour. Although the house contains few of Ade's literary relics (most of these are at Purdue University), it does have much of his original furniture, bric-a-brac, antiques, and objets d'art.

Crawfordsville

Ben-Hur Museum–General Lew Wallace Study. East Pike Street and Wallace Avenue. Apr. 10–Nov. 10, daily except Tues., 10:30–noon, 1:30–5, Sun. 1:30–5 only; closed holidays. Small admission.

Crawfordsville is sometimes referred to as the Athens of the Hoosier State because an unusual number of authors lived here at one time or another, including Meredith Nicholson, a prominent novelist of the early twentieth century and author of *The House of a Thousand Candles* (1905) and *A Hoosier Chronicle* (1912); the playwright Kenyon Nicholson (no relation to Meredith); and Maurice Thompson, author of *Alice of Old Vincennes* (see Vincennes). Most famous in his time of all the Crawfordsville writers was Lew Wallace.

Born in Brookville, Indiana, in 1827, Wallace moved to Crawfordsville in 1853. He was from a prominent family—his father had been governor of Indiana—and he practiced law before going to serve in the Mexican War. He was a general in the Union army during the Civil War, governor of the New Mexico Territory from 1878 to 1881, and minister to Turkey from 1881 to 1885. During his very active life he found time to write numerous books. His novel *The Fair God* (1873), set in the Mexico of Montezuma and Cortez, was enormously popular, as was a later novel, *The Prince of India* (1893), another historical romance. But Lew Wallace is of course known nowadays for *Ben-Hur: a Tale of the Christ,* a novel set in Rome during the era of the birth of Christianity and written to convey Wallace's belief in the divinity of Jesus. Published in 1880, it became one of the bestselling books of all time, and was translated into dozens of languages.

The Study was built in 1896 after Wallace's own design and under his personal supervision on the grounds of his home. Its style is, let us say, eclectic. The entrance gate was inspired by a French abbey. The Study itself is a two-story red-brick building in Byzantine style resembling (in far smaller scale) Santa Sophia in

Constantinople (a reminder of his time as ambassador there), with a domed roof. An adjoining tower, really a chimney for a fireplace, is Romanesque. A portico is Greek Revival, and above this portico is a frieze with sculptures representing characters from his books.

In this study Wallace spent his last years writing. He started his autobiography soon after it was built, but left it unfinished at his death in 1905. The edifice is now a museum displaying mementos from his extraordinarily varied career: war relics, flags, souvenirs of his travels, plus original manuscripts and drawings done by Wallace, who was also a talented artist. Outside, west of the Study, is a bronze statue of Wallace, a replica of the original in the Hall of Fame in Washington, D.C. It stands on the spot of the "Ben-Hur Beech," the tree under which he wrote part of *Ben-Hur*. Wallace is buried in Oak Hill Cemetery in Crawfordsville; his grave is marked by a large monument.

Geneva

Limberlost State Memorial. 200 East Sixth Street, east of US 27 at south edge of town. Mon.–Sat. 9–5, Sun. 1–5. Small admission.

Limberlost Cabin was the home of Gene Stratton Porter from 1895 to 1913. Born in 1863 on Hopewell Farm near Wabash, Indiana, Gene Stratton married Charles Darwin Porter, a druggist and banker, in 1886. After the birth of their daughter they moved to Geneva, in eastern Indiana, where they built this fourteen-room house at the edge of the Limberlost Swamp. At that time the area was still undeveloped backcountry and appealed to Mrs. Porter, a naturalist, for its unspoiled beauty. She was fascinated by the flora and fauna and keenly studied all the flowers, birds, insects, and wild animals living in Limberlost Swamp. An early advocate of conservation, she wrote several nature books. Her meticulous studies were complemented by her accurate watercolor illustrations of the wildlife, and especially by her remarkable nature photography. In the days of cumbersome cameras that required long exposures, she produced some of the best photographs of birds and animals in their natural environment, sometimes spending hours or even days waiting for just the right moment to capture on a photographic plate a family of nesting birds or a rare wildflower in bloom.

She is, of course, best known for her novels, which incorporate her love of nature, particularly her books set in the Limberlost, *Freckles* (1904) and *A Girl of the Limberlost* (1909), both of which were huge bestsellers. Her books are sentimental stories set in an idealized wilderness, in which descriptions of nature are interwoven with the narrative.

The Limberlost Cabin is built from cedar logs from Wisconsin. The entrance hall, library, and dining room are oak-paneled, and the spacious house also has a conservatory, music room, and six bedrooms, all furnished with original pieces. Porter wrote six novels, four nature books, and numerous magazine articles while living here, and took many photographs, some of which are on display.

In 1913 Limberlost Swamp was drained and much of the wildlife began to disappear. Mrs. Porter wanted to live near a place that still had its natural environment intact and found such a place on the shores of Sylvan Lake, near Rome City (which see). In 1914 the Porters left the Limberlost and moved to their new home.

Greenfield

James Whitcomb Riley Boyhood Home. 250 West Main Street (US 40). May 1–Nov. 1, Mon.–Sat. 10–5. Sun. 1–5. Small admission.

James Whitcomb Riley, the "Hoosier Poet," was born in what is now the kitchen of this typical middle-class Indiana home in 1849. At the time the kitchen was a two-room log cabin, the only structure on the property, but a year later Riley's father, a lawyer, was prosperous enough to build the present ten-room frame house, where the future poet grew up. Much of the woodwork was done by Riley's father and many original pieces of furniture and family belongings are in the house.

This house and the town of Greenfield are the locales of his famous dialect poems, which were first published in the Indianapolis *Journal*. His ability to capture the local speech in folksy and humorous verse caught the fancy of the public, and he became one of the most successful writers of his day. The publication of *The Old Swimmin' Hole and 'Leven More Poems* in 1883 made him rich. This volume contained what is probably his most famous poem, "When the Frost Is on the Punkin." Material for "The Raggedy Man," "Little Orphant Annie," and many others came from the ordinary people, local folklore, and familiar and homey surroundings of his small-town boyhood in a village that at the time was just one step away from the wide frontier. In Riley Park (on US 40 near the junction with SR 9), which now has a real swimming pool, is the original "old swimmin' hole."

After the Civil War, the Riley family lost its money and had to move to a smaller house. James vowed he would buy back the house someday, and he did, in 1893, the same year he took up permanent residence in Lockerbie Street in Indianapolis (which see). He insisted on preserving the house as much as possible in the condition in which he remembered it as a boy, just as his poetry preserves a rural life that no longer exists.

A statue of James Whitcomb Riley stands in the courthouse square of Greenfield. It was paid for by funds contributed by the schoolchildren of Indiana.

Every year in early October Greenfield holds a Riley Festival, at the time when "the frost is on the punkin." This includes a parade, dramatic productions, arts and crafts exhibits, go-cart races, and an old fiddlers' contest—a real piece of small-town nostalgia. For information contact Chamber of Commerce, 110 South State Street, Greenfield, IN 46140.

Indianapolis

James Whitcomb Riley Home. 528 Lockerbie Street. Tues.–Sat. 10–4, Sun. 12–4. Admission.

James Whitcomb Riley, who was a lifelong bachelor, moved into this house in 1893 as a paying guest of Major and Mrs.

Charles L. Holstein, longtime friends of his. Riley, in fact, had been friends with Mrs. Holstein's father, John R. Nickum, who built the house in 1872. Not far from downtown Indianapolis, it is one of the best preservations of a Victorian mansion in the country and is a Registered National Historic Landmark. The house is on a charming two-block-long street: "Such a dear little street it is, nestled away / From the noise of the city and heat of the day," Riley wrote. Here he lived comfortably and happily without the responsibility of looking after the household, and he was able to travel, go on his famous lecture tours, and make trips to his hometown of Greenfield (which see).

Even without the literary association, the Riley home is worth a visit. It is a fine example of a late-Victorian upper-class dwelling. Made of solid brick, it has a stone foundation and slate roof. Hand-carved solid woodwork abounds, and there are marble fireplaces throughout the house. Crystal chandeliers imported from Europe, originally for gas but converted to electricity, hang from the ceilings, the stairwell balustrade rises in a continuous piece from first floor to attic, and some of the ceilings are hand-painted by fine artists. Wall-to-wall carpeting complements the ornate Victorian furniture, and fine china and silver are displayed in the sideboard of the dining room.

Riley's room is arranged as it was when he lived here. On his desk lies his pen; his suits are in the closet, and a hat is on the bed. There is also a wicker invalid's chair, which Riley needed after he suffered a stroke. A self-portrait hangs on the wall—Riley was a talented illustrator—and there is also a portrait of his friend Booth Tarkington. Downstairs in the library, Riley's favorite room, are his own books, as well as those of the Holstein family, his easy chair, and a portrait of Riley and one of another literary friend, Joel Chandler Harris, author of the Uncle Remus stories. In the upstairs hall is an exhibit of Riley's papers and personal items.

James Whitcomb Riley died in this house on July 22, 1916, and was buried in Crown Hill Cemetery in Indianapolis. Mrs. Holstein died in October of the same year. Upon her death a group of Riley's friends, which included Booth Tarkington, George Ade, and Meredith Nicholson, purchased the house from Mrs. Holstein's estate and held it until the James Whitcomb Riley Memorial Association was formed in 1921. Thus, the house was never allowed to come into the hands of a stranger or fall into disrepair, but was carefully preserved from the start. When the Lockerbie Street house was opened to the public the first hostess was Katie Kindell, who had been the Holsteins' housekeeper for many years and had known Riley personally.

Two other literary landmarks in Indianapolis are private and not open to the public. Booth Tarkington lived in the English Tudor house at **4270 North Meridian Street;** the house was built in 1910. Meredith Nicholson, author of the bestselling *The House of a Thousand Candles*, built the Georgian house at **1500 North Delaware Street** in 1904.

Rome City

Gene Stratton Porter State Memorial. On the shores of Sylvan Lake, near Rome City. Mon.–Sat. 9–11:45, 1–4:45, Sun. 1–4:45. Small admission; free admission to grounds and picnic area.

When Limberlost Swamp in Geneva, Indiana (which see), was drained, Gene Stratton Porter and her family built a new home here in an unspoiled natural setting and called it "the cabin in Wildflower Woods." She lived here from 1914 to 1921. The two-story house is built of cedar and native stone, its rustic style blending in with the beauty of the natural surroundings. The "cabin" is by no means "primitive," however. There are six rooms plus bath and darkroom downstairs, and seven bedrooms and bath upstairs. The entrance hall is paneled in red-toned wild cherry wood, and maple and pine paneling decorate the upstairs rooms. The living room fireplace is notable for the miniature carved Aztec heads set into the stonework. These were collected by Mr. Porter, and some other Indian artifacts from his collection are displayed in cabinets in the entrance hall. Many of the Porters' original furnishings are preserved here, and personal memorabilia, including Mrs. Porter's books, are also on view.

As a naturalist as well as a writer, Mrs. Porter took great care to develop the flora and fauna of the grounds. She helped transplant thousands of plants along the lakeshore, nurturing the rarer specimens in the conservatory of the house. Deadwood was cut away and new trees planted. She also laid out a flower garden near the house which can still be enjoyed by the visitor; the beds were all planted under her personal direction. The Memorial now consists of thirteen of the original 150 acres; the visitor can also walk through the orchards and arbor and along the scenic paths Mrs. Porter designed.

While in residence at Wildflower Woods Porter continued her wildlife studies and her nature photography. Already a famous writer, she completed three more novels here—*Michael O'Halloran* (1915), *A Daughter of the Land* (1918), and *Her Father's Daughter* (1921)—another nature book, *Homing with the Birds* (1919), and a children's book, *Morning Face* (1916). Around this time Hollywood started adapting her novels for films. *The Harvester* was filmed in and around the cabin in Wildflower Woods. Mrs. Porter decided to make her own movies from her books and in 1920 moved out to California, although she continued to visit her Indiana home. Altogether, seven films were based on her works in the days of silent movies. On December 6, 1924, Gene Stratton Porter died in an automobile accident in Los Angeles at the age of fifty-six.

Terre Haute

Birthplace of Paul Dresser. Fairbanks Park on Dresser Drive. Apr.–Oct., Sun.–Fri. 1–4, closed Sat. and holidays. Free.

Paul Dresser, the composer of "On the Banks of the Wabash" (the Indiana state song), "My Gal Sal," and many other hit songs of the Gay Nineties, was born in this small workingman's home in 1858. Originally located at 318 South Second Street, it was moved to its present location in 1963 and was opened to the public in 1966. In 1967 it was designated a State Shrine and Memorial and was included in the National Register of Historic Places in 1973. The house is typical of the kind the working people of Indiana lived in before the Civil War. Its five rooms are furnished with pieces all dating prior to 1865.

Paul Dresser was the older brother of Theodore Dreiser (who retained the original spelling of the family name). Dreiser was born in Terre Haute in 1871, but not in this house (his birthplace is not extant). Dreiser grew up in poverty in Indiana, in an emotionally turbulent atmosphere punctuated by religious bigotry. By the time he entered Indiana University, which he attended for a year, he was filled with a sense of rebellion and a yearning for independence, and left Indiana to begin his writing career as a newspaperman in St. Louis, Chicago, Pittsburgh, and New York. His autobiographical *A Hoosier Holiday,* published in 1916, tells of his early life in Indiana.

Vincennes

Maurice Thompson Birthplace. On Vincennes University campus. Included in tour arranged through Log Cabin Tourist Center on campus at North First Street and College Avenue, open daily 9–5.

Vincennes, founded by the French on the banks of the Wabash in 1732, is one of the oldest cities west of the Alleghenies. The British took control in 1763, and Colonel George Rogers Clark took Fort Sackville at Vincennes from the British in 1779. This decisive victory prevented the British from keeping the Colonials out of the Old Northwest Territory, and by the Northwest Ordinance of 1787 the entire "Ohio country" was brought under American control. When Ohio became a state in 1800 the Indiana Territory was formed, with Vincennes as its capital.

Maurice Thompson (1844–1901), the Indiana author, wrote a historical romance called *Alice of Old Vincennes,* very popular in its time, about Vincennes in the days of the Revolutionary War. It is a fictionalized version of the true story of Alice Roussillon (whose house stood at Second and Barnett Streets). When the British seized Fort Vincennes (later Sackville) from the French,

Alice rescued the tricolor and hid it so it would not fall into British hands. Years later, Alice had the honor of raising a new American flag over the fort.

Thompson's birthplace, a one-room frame cabin, was originally at Fairfield, Franklin County, Indiana, a site now covered by the Brookville Reservoir. The house was acquired, moved, and restored in 1967 by Vincennes University.

A number of other historical sites are open to the public in Vincennes on its "mile of history." The **George Rogers Clark Memorial,** in a National Historical Park, is a columned rotunda dedicated in 1936, built on the site of old Fort Sackville; murals explain the Clark expedition of 1778–79. The **Indiana Territorial Capitol** is a small two-story frame building erected in 1800 where the legislature of the newly formed Indiana Territory met. **Grouseland** was the mansion of William Henry Harrison, the territory's governor and the ninth President of the United States. The **Western Sun Office** is a replica of the print shop of the territory's first newspaper, established in 1804.

The **Log Cabin Tourist Center** on the Vincennes University Campus has complete information about tours of these and other historic sites in Vincennes. During the summer a Trailblazer Train (an open-air bus) takes visitors on a guided tour of historic Vincennes for a small fee.

The **Brute Library** (behind the cathedral at Second and Church Streets; daily 10–5; small admission) was begun in 1840 and is the oldest library in Indiana. It has a famous collection of rare books and documents, some dating from the fifteenth century.

IOWA

Iowa appears as the locale of some of the stories in Hamlin Garland's *Main-Travelled Roads,* realistic tales that depict the life of the prairie farmers of the mid- and late nineteenth century. Garland, who spent part of his boyhood on a farm in Iowa, also wrote of life on an Iowa homestead in *A Son of the Middle Border* and *A Daughter of the Middle Border.* (See West Salem, Wisconsin, for more on Garland.)

Iowa has produced some interesting local color writing. The turn-of-the-century writer Alice French, who wrote under the name Octave Thanet, spent her childhood in Davenport, and later spent summers there; the town served as the setting for *Stories of a Western Town.* Ruth Suckow (1892–1960), born in Hawarden, Iowa, was known for her realistic stories and novels of midwestern life. Her first and best-known book is *Country People* (1924), about an Iowa farming family. *Iowa Interiors* (1926) is a collection of short stories set primarily in rural Iowa. *The Bonney Family* and *The Folks,* among others, are also studies of the people of Iowa. Another writer popular in the 1920s was Josephine Herbst, who was born in Sioux City in 1897. *Nothing Is Sacred* (1928) is a novel realistically portraying family life in a midwestern town, and *The Executioner Waits* (1934) also uses midwestern material for background. Bess Streeter Aldrich (1881–1954) was born in Cedar Falls, the daughter of pioneer parents. Her novel *Song of the Years* is about pioneer Iowa. In Overman Park in Cedar Falls is a replica of the cabin of Jacob Hoffman, the model for the Wayne Lockwood character in the book. (See also Nebraska.)

Phil Stong wrote a famous piece of Americana, *State Fair,* laid in Des Moines. Herbert Quick's trilogy that begins with *Van-*

demark's Folly gives a realistic picture of Iowa pioneer life. MacKinlay Kantor, author of *Andersonville*, was born in Webster City. Several of his books are set in Iowa, including *Happy Land* and *Spirit Lake*, an account of a massacre of a group of settlers in the 1850s near Spirit Lake, Iowa. Wallace Stegner, noted for his books about the West and rural life, is a native Iowan, received degrees from the University of Iowa in Iowa City, and began his career with a novella set in Iowa entitled *Remembering Laughter*.

Several writers not generally associated with the Midwest had Iowa origins. Carl Van Vechten, known principally for his sophisticated and witty novels about the New York of the 1920s, was born in Iowa. His novel *The Tattooed Countess* (1924) takes place in the Iowa of his youth, around the turn of the century. Susan Glaspell, the novelist and playwright, and founder with her husband, George Cram Cook, of the Provincetown Players, was born in Davenport and worked on newspapers in Des Moines for a time. Her novel *Judd Rankin's Daughter* (1945) has an Iowa setting.

Keokuk

Samuel Clemens, before he became Mark Twain, lived in Keokuk from 1854 until the fall of 1856. He had worked as a printer in Hannibal, Missouri (which see) for his brother Orion. In 1853 the eighteen-year-old Sam, always restless, took off and worked his way east as an itinerant printer in St. Louis, New York City, and Philadelphia. He came back in the summer of 1854 and joined Orion in Keokuk, the first town in Iowa up the Mississippi from Hannibal. Orion had set up a printing business here, and Sam again worked for him. When Sam began his wanderings once more he wrote some comic letters for the Keokuk *Saturday Post* signed Thomas Jefferson Snodgrass; these were in the comic dialect, with atrocious grammar and spelling, that was extremely popular at that time. It was just after he left Keokuk that he met Horace Bixby on a Mississippi riverboat and became an apprentice pilot.

The **Keokuk River Museum** in Victory Park, at the foot of Johnson Street (open mid-Apr.–Oct., Mon.–Sat. 9–5, Sun. and holidays 10–6; small admission) is an old Mississippi stern-wheel steamboat, the *Geo. M. Verity*. Inside are items of historical interest relating to the upper Mississippi River valley. The exhibits and the steamboat itself evoke the period when Mark Twain spent two years of his youth here.

KANSAS

Kansas was home for Dorothy in L. Frank Baum's *The Wonderful Wizard of Oz*. But before Kansas was the peaceful farm state on the prairie that Dorothy wants to come home to, it was the beginning of the Wild West, with towns like Abilene, Wichita, and Dodge City and characters like Wyatt Earp, Doc Holliday, Bat Masterson, and Wild Bill Hickok. Dodge City, one of the most notorious towns on the frontier in the late nineteenth century, now has a reconstruction of the old main street and Boot Hill. Stanley Vestal's *Dodge City* is an excellent account of this town. Wichita has a complex of buildings called Cowtown (1717 Sim Park Drive; open spring through fall) that depicts the town as it was in the late 1800s. And Abilene has Old Abilene Town (201 Southeast Sixth Street), a replica of Abilene in the old cattle boom days. Innumerable Westerns have been written about this era in Kansas history.

E. W. Howe (1853–1937), author of *The Story of a Country Town* (1882), considered the first American naturalist novel, was born in Indiana and grew up in Missouri, but spent most of his adult life in Kansas. In 1877 he started the *Globe* in Atchison, after having published a paper by that name in two other places. In 1905 he bought a farm about two miles south of Atchison, naming it Potato Hill, and in 1911 he moved there to live all of the time and became known as "the Sage of Potato Hill." He began publishing *E. W. Howe's Monthly* and continued to write stories, articles, and editorials. In 1920 *The Anthology of Another Town* came out; it was a collection of stories that like his most famous novel has a midwestern small-town background. William Allen White (see below) was a friend and admirer of Howe.

Kansas's most illustrious literary personage was William Allen White, who spent his life in Emporia (which see) and became world-renowned as a journalist and author.

Paul I. Wellman worked on newspapers in Kansas for twenty-five years, in Wichita and Kansas City, and is known for his books about life in the West. His history of the Indian wars, *Death on the Prairie* (1934) is considered a classic. His series of four novels about the Kansas town of "Jericho" traces the history of that community from frontier days to the contemporary period. The tetralogy consists of *The Bowl of Brass* (1944), *The Walls of Jericho* (1947), *The Chain* (1949), and *Jericho's Daughters* (1956).

The playwright William Inge was born in Independence in 1913. His poignant Pulitzer Prize-winning play *Picnic* (1953) is set in a Kansas town, and his comedy *Bus Stop* takes place in "a small Kansas town about thirty miles west of Kansas City."

Langston Hughes spent part of his boyhood in Kansas; his first novel, *Not Without Laughter* is about a black family in a Kansas town, and his autobiography *The Big Sea* has episodes in Kansas.

Emporia

William Allen White (1869–1944), born in Emporia, attended the University of Kansas and worked on newspapers in Topeka and Kansas City. In 1895 he purchased the *Emporia Gazette*. His 1896 editorial "What's the Matter with Kansas?" was a plea against Populism and made him and his newspaper nationally known. He continued to express his liberal Republican views in brilliant editorials that earned him the epithet "the Sage of Emporia." He epitomized small-town America with his "grass-roots" political opinions, reflected not only in his journalism but in his fiction, which includes the short-story collections *The Court of Boyville* and *In Our Town* and the novels *A Certain Rich Man* and *In the Heart of a Fool,* all with Kansas settings. "Mary White," his tribute to his teenage daughter, who had been killed in a riding accident, is a famous and moving essay that is frequently anthologized. White won the Pulitzer Prize for editorial writing in 1923. The following year a collection of his newspaper writings was published under the title *The Editor and His People,* and in 1937 another collection appeared entitled *Forty Years on Main Street.* His autobiography, published posthumously in 1946, was hailed for its reportorial brilliance and its sensitive personal narrative, and was praised as a lasting document of the history of the American Middle West.

The *Emporia Gazette* is still published in Emporia. The newspaper building at 517 Merchant Street has an exhibit of William Allen White mementos, and a tour of the plant is available on request (building open Mon.–Fri. 8–5, Sat. 8–noon; closed Sun. and holidays; tours Mon.–Fri. by appointment only; telephone 316-342-4800 one day in advance; free).

Red Rocks, the Colorado sandstone home of William Allen White, is at 927 Exchange Street. It is privately owned and not open to the public, but its interesting Victorian Gothic design makes it worth viewing from the outside.

Peter Pan Park, at Kansas Avenue and Neosho Street, was donated by White and his wife as a memorial to their daughter. The park (open daily 8 a.m.–11 p.m.) has picnic grounds and a swimming pool, and is presided over by a bronze bust of William Allen White by the noted sculptor Jo Davidson.

The **Emporia Public Library** (118 East Sixth Avenue at Market Street) has a complete file of the *Emporia Gazette* and a collection of White's books.

MICHIGAN

Several areas in Michigan have significant literary associations. In Sault Ste. Marie, one of the oldest cities on the North American continent and site of the Soo Locks between Lake Superior and Lake Huron, is a house at 705 East Portage Avenue that was occupied by Henry Rowe Schoolcraft from 1827, when it was built, until 1833. (The house, altered from its original appearance, is on the grounds of the Edison Sault Power Company and is not open to the public at the present time.) Schoolcraft (1793–1864) was an explorer (he discovered the source of the Mississippi River in 1832), geologist, and ethnologist, and served as an Indian agent. He was married to the daughter of a Chippewa chief, and from her and from his own research he gathered voluminous material on Indian lore and legends. He was the first white man to translate Indian poetry into English and wrote a number of influential books about the Indians, notably *Algic Researches, Comprising Inquiries Respecting the Mental Characteristics of the North American Indians,* and *History, Condition, and Prospects of the Indian Tribes of the United States,* in which two books Henry Wadsworth Longfellow found his sources for *Hiawatha.* Longfellow wrote in his Author's Note to the poem:

> Into this old tradition [of a personage of miraculous birth, who was sent among the people to clear the rivers, forests, and fishing-grounds and to teach them peace] I have woven other curious Indian legends, drawn chiefly from the various and valuable writings of Mr. Schoolcraft, to whom the literary world is greatly indebted for his indefatigable zeal in rescuing from oblivion so much of the legendary lore of the Indians.
>
> The scene of the poem is among the Ojibways on the south-

ern shore of Lake Superior, in the region between the Pictured
Rocks and the Grand Sable.

It should be noted that Longfellow erred by confusing the
Iroquois Hiawatha and the Chippewa Manabozo. Hiawatha being
an Iroquois, the poem should have been set in New York State
rather than on the Michigan upper peninsula to be technically
accurate. But of course, historical verity isn't the point of
Hiawatha. Longfellow himself said he wanted to weave together
the beautiful traditions of many Indian tribes. The **Indian Dormi-
tory** on **Mackinac Island** (which see), a restoration of an 1838
structure with Indian and archaeological exhibits, has a mural
portraying scenes from *Hiawatha* (open daily in summer, 11–5).

The upper peninsula, incidentally, is the setting for quite a
different work of literature, also. *Anatomy of a Murder,* the
bestselling novel by Robert Traver (pseudonym of John Voelker,
a former Michigan supreme court justice), takes place in Marquette County. The film starring James Stewart was filmed on
location in and around the town of Marquette, where the courthouse is situated.

Some interesting early realistic writing about Michigan was
done by Caroline Stansbury Kirkland (1801–64), who used the
pen name Mrs. Mary Clavers. She traveled with her missionary
husband to Michigan and settled in the village of Pinckney. She
wrote three semifictional, satirical books that offer unflattering
portraits of the crude pioneer life: *A New Home—Who'll Follow?*
(1839), *Forest Life* (1842), and *Western Clearings* (1845).

The Michigan-born adventure novelist Stewart Edward White
(1873–1946) wrote several books set in the state; *The Blazed Trail*
was based on his experiences in a Michigan lumber camp.

In modern times, Michigan claims Ring Lardner as a native
son. He was born in Niles, and many of his stories reflect his
small-town midwestern background.

The automobile industry centered around Detroit has been the
subject of a number of recent trashy novels, which shall go unnamed. The city also provides the locale for one of Joyce Carol
Oates's most powerful novels, *Them* (1969), a tragic tale of two
generations of a white slum family. The novel culminates in a
hallucinatory vision of the riots of 1967. (Unfortunately, such
stories about Detroit do not lend themselves to literary touring.)

Little Traverse Bay area

The summer vacation area around Little Traverse Bay in the northwestern part of the lower peninsula was where Ernest Hemingway spent many summers as a child and a young man. Carlos Baker begins his biography of Hemingway thus:

> As soon as it was safe for the boy to travel, they bore him away to the northern woods. It was a long and complicated journey for a child only seven weeks old. From the suburban town of Oak Park, Illinois, they took the train to Chicago, a horse cab to the pier on Lake Michigan, the steamer *Manitou* to Harbor Springs on Little Traverse Bay, the curving tracks of the small railroad to the depot in Petoskey, an even smaller branch line to the foot of Bear Lake, and at last a rowboat to the shore-front property that Dr. Ed Hemingway had bought from Henry Bacon the summer before. They were going to build a summer cottage and they had come to complete the arrangements.

This was in 1899. A year later the cottage, christened Windemere, on Walloon Lake, was occupied by the Hemingway family. (The house is still privately owned.) Here Ernest and his brothers and sisters spent happy summer days on the beach. Today the lake is still clear and lovely.

Ernest returned to the area in 1919 when he came back from the First World War, still recuperating from leg wounds. He had already written some stories and took up the pen again when he settled in at a friend's house in Horton Bay on Lake Charlevoix, since he had decided he wanted to be independent and did not want to stay with his family at Windemere Cottage. His experiences during this summer found their way into some of the stories of his first two books, *Three Stories and Ten Poems* (1923) and *In Our Time* (1924), the latter written mostly in Paris. The notorious "Up in Michigan" was included in the first volume but was discreetly deleted from the second collection because it dealt graphically with sexual intercourse. It takes place in Horton Bay and is most likely based on an incident in that summer of 1919 when Hemingway and a waitress he had met "mutually seduced" one another.

Other stories with Michigan settings are "The Doctor and the Doctor's Wife," "The End of Something," and "The Three-Day Blow." In "Indian Camp" Nick Adams, Hemingway's youthful alter ego, is introduced to violence when he accompanies his doctor father, and "Big Two-Hearted River," in which Nick takes a solitary hiking and fishing trip to recuperate from his war wounds, is based on a camping trip Ernest made late in the summer of 1919 to the upper peninsula.

In October 1919 Hemingway decided to move to Petoskey. He rented a room in a boardinghouse at 602 State Street, which still stands. Petoskey provided him with the setting for his first novel, *The Torrents of Spring* (1926), a parody of Sherwood Anderson. He stayed in Petoskey until December, giving a talk in that month about his wartime exploits at a meeting of the Ladies' Aid Society at the Petoskey Public Library. Around Christmas he returned to Oak Park and then went to Toronto to stay with a family he had met in Petoskey. He returned to Michigan in the summer of 1920, and after a row with his mother moved into a boardinghouse in Boyne City. At the end of that summer he went to Chicago, where he met Hadley Richardson, his first wife, whom he married in a church (now gone) in the village of Horton Bay.

Petoskey today is a posh summer resort with elegant boutiques. Harbor Springs, Walloon Lake, Lake Charlevoix, and the other towns and villages around Little Traverse Bay make up one of the finest resort areas in the country, with boating and fishing in the clear waters that first gave Ernest Hemingway the love of sport, adventure, and the outdoors.

Mackinac Island

Mackinac Island has been a famous resort since the nineteenth century, and its pristine ambience is retained by banning automobiles on the island; transportation is by horse and carriage or by bicycle. Before it was a resort, however, it was a key location in the struggle between the French and British for control of the fur trade. After Wolfe's victory at Quebec, the English took over from the French; the island was turned over to the Americans after the Revolutionary War, was seized by the British in the War of 1812, and finally was returned to the United States.

Constance Fenimore Woolson (1840–94), a talented novelist and short-story writer who was greatly admired by Henry James, wrote a novel called *Anne,* published in 1882. Like many other well-to-do people, she spent several summers here with her family, and she became interested in the history of the island. *Anne* takes place in the old Great Lakes settlement of Fort Mackinac and is a realistic portrayal of the life of a young girl there. The novel also gives a picture of the French settlers and those of mixed white and Indian blood who lived on the island.

A bronze memorial, called **"Anne's Tablet,"** on Woolson Rampart, East Bluff, was erected in honor of the author. It shows the heroine of the book reaching up toward a branch of a tree. (Woolson also wrote *Castle Nowhere,* a collection of stories about French settlers in the Great Lakes region.)

Old Fort Mackinac, in Mackinac Island State Park, was erected in 1780, and has ramparts, blockhouses, and cannon, plus exhibits on the island's history (open daily in summer 9:30–6, Labor Day through Sept., 10–4; closed rest of year; admission). Other historical buildings on the island include the American Fur Co. Trading Post (in the village of Mackinac Island) and the Benjamin Blacksmith Shop (Market Street), a replica of an 1880s forge.

MINNESOTA

The epic story of the Swedish migration to Minnesota and neighboring states is told in the Swedish novelist Vilhelm Moberg's "emigrant" tetralogy, the first volume of which is *The Emigrants* (made into a Swedish film). Relics of the early Swedish settlers can be seen in small museums throughout the state and at the **American Swedish Institute** in **Minneapolis** (2600 Park Avenue South).

The folklore figure of Paul Bunyan has its origins in the lumber camps of the Great Lakes region. Bemidji, Minnesota, claims to be the "birthplace" of Paul Bunyan, and has giant statues of Paul and Babe the Blue Ox adjacent to an Information Center (Third Street and Bemidji Avenue) with exhibits on the Paul Bunyan legend. The folk hero has been the subject of numerous collections of stories.

Minnesota is the birthplace of two of America's most important writers: F. Scott Fitzgerald came from St. Paul and Sinclair Lewis from the small town of Sauk Centre (see individual entries).

Minneapolis

Minnehaha Park. Minnehaha Parkway and Hiawatha Avenue South (on the banks of the Mississippi River).

In Longfellow's poem, Hiawatha journeys to the "land of the Dacotahs" to woo Minnehaha, or Laughing Water:

> And he journeyed without resting,
> Till he heard the cataract's laughter,
> Heard the Falls of Minnehaha
> Calling to him through the silence.

Minnehaha Falls, in Minnehaha Park, is a cascade that purports to be the "laughing water" of the poem. (*Minne* is actually a Sioux word for water—hence the semionomatopoeic name Minnehaha—and Minneapolis is *minne* plus *polis,* Greek for "city.") A statue of Hiawatha and Minnehaha stands in the park.

Guthrie Theater. Vineland Place (1 block south of junction of US 12 and US 169). Season runs June–Feb. Check locally for information on programs and tickets (box office telephone: 612-377-2224).

The Guthrie Theater, which opened in 1963 under the direction of Sir Tyrone Guthrie, has become internationally famous for its high-quality productions of classic and contemporary plays. Its resident professional company presents about seven or eight plays annually. Guthrie's idea was to establish a repertory theater in the Midwest, away from New York, to give the people of the heartland an opportunity to see live theater, and especially the classics, performed by talented professional actors. Guthrie left after three seasons to go on to other projects, although he returned on several occasions to direct (he died in 1971).

The Guthrie maintains a consistent standard of excellence in its acting, directing, and physical production, and appeals to a wide audience, who come to see Shakespeare, Ibsen, Brecht, and other great playwrights, as well as some interesting lesser dramatists, performed in a beautiful theater with an open framework façade that encloses the glass front of the building. The 1437-seat auditorium has an open thrust stage, with no seat more than fifty-two feet from the center of the stage.

St. Paul

F. Scott Fitzgerald was born on September 24, 1896, in a house on Laurel Avenue in St. Paul. Arthur Mizener, in *The Far Side of Paradise*, his biography of Fitzgerald, details the author's early years in St. Paul as the son of a father from "good stock" who had little money. When Fitzgerald was two his family moved to Buffalo, New York, but they returned to St. Paul when Scott was twelve. The family didn't have as much money as those they associated with, but Scott went to school with the children of the best St. Paul families. The Fitzgeralds moved several times from one house to another during a period of a number of years. They lived at **294 Laurel Avenue,** then **514 Holly Avenue,** then **509** and **499 Holly.** They then moved to **593 Summit Avenue,** one of a number of row houses known as Summit Terrace featuring bay windows, octagonal turrets, and recessed doorways. In 1918 the family moved to **599 Summit Avenue,** in the same group of houses. As Mizener points out, Summit Avenue is St. Paul's show street, but the row houses were near Dale Street, and Dale Street is where Summit becomes just an ordinary street. Thus, in Mizener's words, "as Fitzgerald grew up, his family moved gradually around the periphery of St. Paul's finest residential district, settling finally at the end of its best street."

Fitzgerald's adolescence in St. Paul found its way into a number of his short stories, particularly the Basil Duke Lee stories and some of the stories in *All the Sad Young Men*. His first novel was written in his third-floor-front room at 599 Summit in the summer of 1919 after he got out of the army (he had already met Zelda Sayre in Montgomery, Alabama). The book was *This Side of Paradise,* published in 1920. After they were married, and after that crazy first year in New York and Europe, Scott and Zelda (who was then pregnant) came to live in St. Paul. They stayed for about a year, from late summer 1921 to October 1922. It was during this period that Fitzgerald completed *The Beautiful and the Damned.*

None of the places Fitzgerald lived in in St. Paul is open to the public, but a walk or drive around the Summit Hill neighborhood, which is still a neighborhood of beautiful homes, is worthwhile.

Incidentally, Sinclair Lewis spent the winter of 1917–18 in St. Paul, in a large rented house at **516 Summit Avenue.**

Sauk Centre

Sinclair Lewis Interpretive Center. At junction of US 71 and I-94. Daily; Memorial Day–Labor Day, 10–6, rest of year, 10–4. Free.

Sinclair Lewis Boyhood Home. 612 Sinclair Lewis Avenue, 3½ blocks west of downtown traffic light. Memorial Day–Labor Day, Mon.–Sat. 10–6, Sun. 1–6, rest of year by appointment. Admission.

When Harry Sinclair Lewis was born in Sauk Centre, Minnesota, on February 7, 1885, the town was not yet thirty years old, having risen on the empty prairie in 1857. The red-haired gawky boy, who acquired the nickname Red, did not have a happy childhood. He was not abused, certainly, but his father, the town doctor, was a remote and solemn man, rigid in his habits, and his mother died when he was six (his father remarried a year later a woman whom Mark Schorer, in his biography *Sinclair Lewis: An American Life,* describes as "kindly and sensible . . . if by no means abundantly open in her affections"). Young Harry had few friends, and the predominant mood of his boyhood seems to have been loneliness.

Sauk Centre is the Gopher Prairie of Lewis's novel *Main Street.* Mark Schorer called its publication in 1920 "the most sensational event in twentieth-century American publishing history." *Main Street* was by no means the first book to attack the narrowness and philistinism of small-town life; the "attack on the village" had already been launched by writers like Sherwood Anderson and Edgar Lee Masters. But Main Street was certainly the most widely read and controversial of these works. In it, Carol Kennicott, the wife of the local doctor, rebels against the dullness of her life in Gopher Prairie and longs for refinement and culture. Lewis's satire and indictment of Gopher Prairie society and thinking, of American small-town provincialism, established him as a major American novelist.

It is, of course, slightly ironic that the model for the town that Lewis excoriated now prides itself on being Lewis's hometown. The main drag now proclaims itself the "Original Main Street," and the street where his boyhood home stands has been renamed in his honor. Lewis, however, did not hate Sauk Centre. He returned for visits a number of times, and it should be remembered that *Main Street* has a good number of affectionately portrayed characters in it as well as sharp satire. Yet in a sense, Sauk Centre has lived up to the satire in the book by turning negative criticism into positive thinking, honoring its most famous citizen, who made Sauk Centre itself famous for the wrong reasons. Lewis would have been amused, as he might have been at some of the absurder aspects of his funeral, which took place in Sauk Centre in 1951 after his ashes had been delivered from Italy, where he died. Schorer describes the almost comical ceremonies that ended with Lewis's brother pouring the ashes out of the urn into the grave in the cemetery east of town only to have some of them be blown away by a sudden gust of wind.

As you come into town, the **Sinclair Lewis Interpretive Center** is on the left, where I-94 and US 71 (Main Street) come together. Here an eighteen-minute slide show on Lewis's life is shown, and original manuscripts, letters, and other Lewis memorabilia are exhibited. There is also a research library open to scholars.

A short drive up Main Street and a turn to the left takes you to the **Boyhood Home,** a Registered Historic Landmark. The modest L-shaped frame house has been meticulously restored. Here Lewis lived with his parents and his brothers Fred and Claude. It has much of the original furniture: heavy late-Victorian pieces, tables covered with fringed cloths, bedrooms with flowered wallpaper. It is ordinary and comfortable, unimaginative and bordering on the ugly. The bathroom, with its original heating pipes, was installed only in 1905, when Lewis had already gone off to Yale, after the residential part of town received a sewage system.

One can easily imagine that the author's sharp satire of the village developed out of irritation at the boredom with life here. It is nevertheless interesting to see the roots of an important American literary figure.

Eugene O'Neill's Tao House, Danville, California

Ruins of Jack London's Wolf House, Glen Ellen, California

Home of John Muir, Martinez, California

Edgar Lee Masters Memorial Museum, Petersburg, Illinois

Vachel Lindsay home, Springfield, Illinois

Ben-Hur Museum–General Lew Wallace Study, Crawfordsville, Indiana

The Study, Gene Stratton Porter State Memorial, Rome City, Indiana

Sinclair Lewis boyhood home, Sauk Centre, Minnesota

Mississippi River at Hannibal, Missouri, Mark Twain's hometown

Laura Ingalls Wilder–Rose Wilder Lane Home and Museum, Mansfield, Missouri

WILDER-LANE HOME AND MUSEUM

Willa Cather's home, Red Cloud, Nebraska

The Study, Hamlin Garland homestead, West Salem, Wisconsin

MISSOURI

Much of the early literature of Missouri combines traits of Southern and Western writing, an obvious result of the state's central location. The Mississippi River flows along its eastern border; the Ozarks, with a rich folklore tradition, rise on the south; and the Missouri River cuts across the state, linking the Mississippi to the great western frontier. The distinctive dialect of eastern Missouri was rendered in John Hay's *Pike County Ballads* (1871), a collection of poems that included "Jim Bludso of the Prairie Belle," about the heroism of a steamboat engineer who saves his passengers when his boat catches fire.

Mississippi River steamboats, of course, were the great obsession of Mark Twain, who dominates Missouri literature, as, indeed, he does American literature itself. His boyhood in Hannibal provided him with rich material and the town is a shrine to him and his characters.

Vance Randolph, a Missourian, studied Ozark Mountain folk and produced several collections of Ozarks lore, including *The Ozarks, Ozark Superstitions, We Always Lie to Strangers,* and the recently published *Pissing in the Snow and Other Ozark Folktales,* consisting of hilarious bawdy stories.

Branson

Shepherd of the Hills Farm. On SR 76, 7 miles west of Branson. Daily, Apr. 1–mid-Nov., 9–6; charge for tour in jeep-drawn conveyance; free admission to grounds.

In the heart of the Ozarks, near the Arkansas border, an area of lakes and large caves (many open to the public), is the Shepherd of the Hills Farm, the setting for *The Shepherd of the Hills* (1907), a popular novel by the minister-author Harold Bell Wright (1872–1944). Wright had come to these hills at the end of the nineteenth century for his health and drew his inspiration for his book about the Ozarks people from his friends and neighbors here. The farm has been preserved as it appears in the novel and is a major tourist attraction in the popular Ozarks vacation region.

A fifty-minute tour in a jeep-drawn vehicle takes the visitor along an old trail to see various spots that play a part in the book. **Old Matt's Cabin** is the original home of the Matthews family of the book, and is furnished with Victorian pieces. **Inspiration Point,** the highest point in Taney County, has a view of more than a hundred miles. It is the spot where Wright camped while writing his book, and now has statues of the principal characters of the novel. **Pete's Cave** is believed to be an entrance to the cave that appears in the book. Also on the grounds of the farm is the **Memorial Museum,** which houses a collection of art, sculpture, and antiques from the Ozarks region as well as the famous Rose O'Neill doll collection.

At **Matt's Mill,** where an old gristmill is still in operating condition, there is the outdoor **Old Mill Theatre,** where in the evenings throughout spring, summer, and early fall a dramatization of *The Shepherd of the Hills* is presented. Acted by local people, the show has become one of the most popular outdoor pageants in the country. Tickets can be purchased at the Shepherd of the Hills Farm; or write the Shepherd of the Hills Historical Society, Branson, MO 65616; or telephone Branson Chamber of Commerce, toll-free: in Missouri, 800-492-7624, out of Missouri, 800-641-7830.

Two other sites associated with the novel but not at the farm are the **Jim Lane Cabin,** the historic homestead of one of the characters, on SR 76, 6 miles west of Branson, and **Uncle Ike's Post Office,** also referred to in the book, on SR 76, 9½ miles west of Branson, beyond the farm.

Florida

Mark Twain Birthplace Memorial Shrine. Mark Twain State Park, about 30 miles southwest of Hannibal on SR 107, via US 24. Mon.–Sat. 10–5; Sun., Memorial Day–Labor Day 12–6, rest of the year 12–5. Small admission.

In his *Autobiography* Mark Twain wrote:

> I was born the 30th of November, 1835, in the almost invisible village of Florida, Monroe County, Missouri. My parents removed to Missouri in the early 'thirties; I do not remember just when, for I was not born then and cared nothing for such things. It was a long journey in those days and must have been a rough and tiresome one. The village contained a hundred people and I increased the population by 1 per cent. It is more than many of the best men in history could have done for a town. It may not be modest in me to refer to this but it is true. There is no record of a person doing as much—not even Shakespeare. But I did it for Florida and it shows that I could have done it for any place—even London, I suppose.
>
> Recently some one in Missouri has sent me a picture of the house I was born in. Heretofore I have always stated that it was a palace but I shall be more guarded now.

Indeed, it was not a palace, but rather a small two-room cabin. Sam Clemens's father was a storekeeper and sometime lawyer, and not too successful at either calling. The Clemens family lived in a number of different houses in Florida before moving to Hannibal in 1839, when Sam was four years old. During his boyhood Sam returned to Florida to spend summers at the farm of his uncle, John A. Quarles; he writes affectionately about these idyllic summers in his *Autobiography*.

The birthplace cabin is now enclosed in a modern building of stone, aluminum, and glass. A unique feature of the shrine is the unusually shaped roof, a hyperbolic paraboloid made of reinforced concrete with an outer surface of white marble chips, which covers the birth house. The shrine also contains a museum with exhibits on Mark Twain, including a riverboat pilothouse, original manuscripts, first editions of Twain's books, and some furniture and small articles from his various homes. In addition, the shrine has a research library. There is also a bust of Mark Twain by the sculptor R. P. Bringhurst. Now exhibited in the shrine, it originally stood on the actual location of the birthplace (which was moved), a short way up the road; the pedestal still stands on this site. A film of Dr. George William Smith as Mark Twain giving a lecture is shown in the museum.

Mark Twain State Park has recreational and camping facilities. For information write Mark Twain State Park, Stoutsville, MO 65283.

Hannibal

Hannibal, Missouri, pervades the writings of Mark Twain. A thriving river town in the 1840s, when young Sam Clemens was growing up, it was a community of clearly defined moral standards but also one with western exuberance. A boy growing up there had an opportunity to observe the commerce of the country go by at the end of his street. Mississippi riverboats plied up and down the river, and the greatest—although frequent—thrill in Hannibal was the cry of "Steamboat a-coming!"

Clemens's boyhood in Hannibal was the fount from which his great works arose, a youth not without its griefs (his father died in 1847, when Sam was eleven), but also with a great deal of fun. Hannibal is nostalgically re-created as the St. Petersburg of *The Adventures of Tom Sawyer* and *The Adventures of Huckleberry Finn*. Huck was modeled on Tom Blankenship, a rogue of a boy Clemens knew in Hannibal, Aunt Polly was based in part on his own mother, and Tom Sawyer was mostly young Sam himself.

Twain describes Hannibal in his *Autobiography:*

> In the small town of Hannibal, Missouri, when I was a boy everybody was poor but didn't know it; and everybody was comfortable and did know it. And there were grades of

society—people of good family, people of unclassified family, people of no family. Everybody knew everybody and was affable to everybody and nobody put on any visible airs; yet the class lines were quite clearly drawn and the familiar social life of each class was restricted to that class. It was a little democracy which was full of liberty, equality and Fourth of July, and sincerely so, too; yet you perceived that the aristocratic taint was there. It was there and nobody found fault with the fact or ever stopped to reflect that its presence was an inconsistency.

He attributes this condition to the greatest flaw in that society:

I suppose that this state of things was mainly due to the circumstance that the town's population had come from slave states and still had the institution of slavery with them in their new home.

As anyone who has read Mark Twain knows, he did not see his boyhood in Hannibal merely as a sunny idyll of youth, but as a pleasant, even wondrous time that nevertheless had its dark side. Twain used Hannibal to create his own myth of American society, as Dixon Wecter's *Sam Clemens of Hannibal,* a detailed examination of Clemens's youth and its relation to his writings, shows.

Clemens had little formal education, attending local schools until shortly after his father's death, when because of his family's straitened circumstances he was apprenticed to a printer. His elder brother Orion set up shop as a newspaper publisher in Hannibal in 1851, and Sam worked as his assistant, setting type and doing odd jobs. It was during this period that Sam contributed some humorous pieces to the *Journal,* amateur efforts in the popular Western dialect of the day. Sam left Hannibal at the age of eighteen as an itinerant printer. He never lived in Hannibal again, but he is certainly all over the place today.

In Hannibal, many buildings associated with Mark Twain have been preserved by the city and are a major tourist attraction in this area of the country. (A brochure with map is available from the Chamber of Commerce, 623 Broadway, P.O. Box 230, Hannibal, MO 63401.)

Mark Twain Boyhood Home and Museum. 208 Hill Street. Daily; June 1–Sept. 1, 8–8; Sept. 2–May 30, 8–5. Free.

Built in 1844 by Sam's father, the boyhood home is a plain, two-story white frame house, flush with the sidewalk on a street that slopes toward the river. It was cheaply constructed and has small rooms and low ceilings. But even the upkeep of this more than modest house was too much for Sam's father, John Marshall Clemens, to bear, and in 1846 reverses in the family's finances forced them to take quarters across the street in the "Pilaster House" (see below). Sometime after the elder Clemens's death, the family moved back into this house. It is now furnished with period pieces and is a Registered National Historic Landmark. Alongside the house is the white board fence that is the site of the annual fence-painting contest held during Tom Sawyer Days (early July), which also includes a frog-jumping contest and raft races.

Adjacent to the boyhood home is the Mark Twain Museum, dedicated in in 1937. Personal articles belonging to Mark Twain, rare books, old photographs, and original Twain manuscripts are exhibited.

Becky Thatcher House. 211 Hill Street. Same schedule as Boyhood Home. Free.

Just across Hill Street from the Clemens home, this house was the residence of Annie Laurie Hawkins, usually called Laura. Laura Hawkins was Sam Clemens's first childhood sweetheart, and he based the character of Becky Thatcher in *Tom Sawyer* on her. Laura Hawkins married a young physician, Dr. James W. Frazer, and lived to the age of ninety-one. (Twain used her name for the heroine of *The Gilded Age,* but only the name, not the character; that belongs to Becky.) In 1908 there was a reunion when Laura Hawkins visited Twain at Stormfield, his home in Connecticut; she came away with many sweet memories and a photograph the author inscribed: "To Laura Frazer, with the love of her earliest sweetheart." The parlor and upstairs bedroom of the house have been restored with authentic period pieces.

Judge Clemens's Law Office. On Hill Street, down the block from Becky Thatcher House. Same schedule as above. Free.

Sam's father served as a justice of the peace in Hannibal. In *Innocents Abroad* Twain tells how one day in 1843 he snuck into his father's deserted office to avoid his father's wrath at his being truant from school. On the floor he discovered a man's corpse; the man had been stabbed in the chest. He writes, "I went out at the window, and I carried the sash along with me; I did not need the sash, but it was handier to take it than it was to leave it, and so I took it." Presumably the corpse was there because as a justice of the peace, the elder Clemens shared responsibility for coroner's inquests. The corpse was that of one James McFarland, murdered in a drunken quarrel by Vincent Hudson. This was the first homicide in the history of Hannibal.

Pilaster House and Grant Drug Store. Southwest corner of Hill and Main Streets. Same schedule as above. Free.

In 1846 the fortunes of the Clemens family hit bottom and they were forced to give up even their meager house on Hill Street. According to Wecter, the Clemenses accepted the invitation of Dr. Orville Grant to live with his family over the drugstore in this building. It is a frame house of two and a half stories with white Greek Revival pilasters on the exterior walls; architecturally the most interesting house in Hannibal, it is also more dignified and of finer construction than the common Hannibal building. It was in this house that John Clemens, Sam's father, died, on March 24, 1847, after a chill developed into pneumonia. After his death, the family moved out of this house and eventually back to their home on Hill Street. The Pilaster House contains a restoration of living quarters of the period of the 1840s, an old-time drugstore, kitchen, and doctor's office.

Tom Sawyer Dioramas. 323 North Main Street. Mar.–Dec., daily. Admission.

These dioramas with three-dimensional miniature figures carved by Art Sieving depict scenes from *The Adventures of Tom Sawyer* and are rather charming.

The block of **Main Street** between Hill Street and Bird Street has commercial buildings that survive from the nineteenth century and that now house craft and antique shops. At the north end of Main Street is **Cardiff Hill,** as it is called in *Tom Sawyer,* originally Holliday's Hill in Twain's day. At the foot of the hill where Sam and his pals played, and where Huck Finn and Tom Sawyer played, too, is a life-size statue of Tom and Huck by sculptor F. C. Hibbard. Steps lead up Cardiff Hill (you can also drive up from an entrance off US 36); at the top is the **Mark Twain Memorial Lighthouse,** built by the city of Hannibal in 1935 to mark the one hundredth anniversary of Mark Twain's birth. It was dedicated as a "monument to undimmed youth." The bridge over the Mississippi River here is called the Mark Twain Memorial Bridge. In **Riverview Park,** high on a bluff overlooking the river just north of town, is a statue of Mark Twain in his later years, looking out over the river he loved.

Two other buildings in Hannibal are also open to the public:

Rockcliffe Mansion. 1000 Bird Street. Daily 9:30–5:30. Guided tours. Closed Thanksgiving, Christmas, New Year's Day. Admission.

This splendid mansion was built by John J. Cruikshank, a lumber magnate, who lived here with his wife and four daughters from 1900 until he died in 1924. After his death the thirty-room house was unoccupied for forty-three years until it was restored and opened to the public. This river estate is constructed and decorated in the art nouveau style that was an innovation at the turn of the century. When Mark Twain made his last visit to Hannibal in 1902 he addressed three hundred guests gathered here from the magnificent stairway, which is flanked by two elaborate electric light fixtures on the newel posts.

Molly Brown House. On Denkler Alley just off US 36. Memorial Day–Labor Day, daily 10–6; rest of year by appointment (telephone 314-221-8979). Small admission.

Although unrelated to Mark Twain, this house is a curiosity in its own right. Built before the Civil War, the house was the birthplace of Margaret Tobin, known as "the Unsinkable Molly Brown," whose husband struck it rich in the Colorado mines (her house in Denver is a museum now), and who earned her sobriquet when she rowed passengers to safety in the *Titanic* disaster. The house has furnishings of the circa-1870 period.

Other activities in Hannibal: The **Twainland Express** (at Third and Hill Streets near the Boyhood Museum) is a trackless train that takes the visitor on a narrated twelve-mile, one-hour tour of Hannibal. It operates daily from mid-May to mid-September, 10–5; admission.

A one-hour riverboat excursion on a stern-wheeler starts from the **Steamboat Landing** at the foot of Center Street; Memorial Day–Labor Day, daily, some weekends in May and September; admission (telephone 314-221-3222 for latest information).

The **Ice House Theatre** (1 Hill Street, 1 block east of Boyhood Home) is a converted nineteenth-century icehouse where a stock company performs plays during the summer months. Tickets are available at the box office or from the Chamber of Commerce. Telephone 314-221-6070 for information and reservations.

Two other attractions are a short drive from Hannibal:

Mark Twain Cave. 2 miles south on SR 79. Daily, Apr.–Oct., 8–8; Nov.–Mar., 8–5. 45-minute guided tour. Admission.

Mark Twain wrote about this cave in several of his books. The cave was known in his day as McDowell's cave, because it was owned by the eccentric Dr. E. D. McDowell. In *Life on the Mississippi,* Twain notes, "In my time the person who then owned it turned it into a mausoleum for his daughter, aged fourteen. The body of this poor child was put in a copper cylinder filled with alcohol, and this was suspended in one of the dismal avenues of the cave." This was McDowell's daughter; apparently he was experimenting to see whether the limestone cavern would "petrify" her body, according to Dixon Wecter's book. This rather macabre story put a sinister, or at least spooky, aspect on the cave for Twain. The most famous reference to the cave in his works is, of course, in *Tom Sawyer,* where it is called McDougal's Cave. Here Tom and Becky get lost and Injun Joe dies, and it is where Tom and Huck find the robbers' loot. Twain's description of the cave in the novel is vivid:

> No man knew the cave: that was an impossible thing. Most
> of the young men knew a portion of it and it was not customary

to venture much beyond this known portion. Tom Sawyer knew as much of the cave as anyone. The procession moved along the main avenue some three-quarters of a mile and then groups and couples began to slip aside into branch avenues, fly along the dismal corridors and take each other by surprise at points where the corridors joined together.

In his *Autobiography* Twain reminisces:

> Many excursion parties came from considerable distances up and down the river to visit the cave. It was miles in extent and was a tangled wilderness of lofty clefts and passages. It was an easy place to get lost in; anybody could do it—including the bats. I got lost in it myself, along with a lady, and our last candle burned down to almost nothing before we glimpsed the search party's lights winding about in the distance.

The cave is a labyrinth of limestone created by water erosion, with a temperature of 52 degrees F. the year round. The visitors' circuit is now electrically lighted, and since there are no steps it is an easy walk past numerous interesting formations. (Parking, picnic grounds, and free nature trails are outside the cave.)

Garth Woodside Mansion. RR 1, via US 61 south; turn east on first road south of Holiday Inn; at second bridge follow signs. Tours daily, May–Oct., 9:30–5:30, Nov.–Apr., 11–4. Admission.

John Garth was a schoolmate of Sam Clemens in Hannibal, the son of the tobacconist who taught Sunday school in the Presbyterian church. Garth married Helen Kercheval, in Twain's words, "one of the prettiest schoolgirls" in the town. After the Civil War Garth prospered in the tobacco business and in banking and became one of Hannibal's leading citizens. In 1871 he built this twenty-room country estate a few miles south of town. It has an impressive flying staircase that rises to the third floor with no visible means of support. Seven hand-carved Italian marble mantels grace the rooms, which are furnished in ornate late-Victorian style. When Twain visited Hannibal in 1882 (during a trip described in the second half of *Life on the Mississippi*) Garth played host to his old boyhood friend. Years later, in 1902, Twain made another trip to Missouri; this time, he records, he saw John's tomb.

Mansfield

Laura Ingalls Wilder–Rose Wilder Lane Home and Museum.
Rocky Ridge Farm, 1 mile east of Mansfield on Business Route
60. May 1–Oct. 15, daily except Sun. 9–4. Admission.

Rocky Ridge Farm was the home of Laura Ingalls Wilder, the
author of the "Little House" books for children, from 1894 until
her death in 1957 at the age of ninety. She and her husband, with
their little daughter Rose, left De Smet, South Dakota (which
see), where the rest of her family remained, to settle on this farm
in the Ozarks. They cleared the land and built their farmhouse
themselves. In her sixties, Mrs. Wilder began writing her famous
series of children's books that chronicle the life of her pioneer
family in Wisconsin, the Dakota territory, Minnesota, and Kansas. The first of the series is *The Little House in the Big Woods,*
followed by *The Little House on the Prairie* and six others. They
are all a record of the true experiences of the family, and the last
book, *These Happy Golden Years,* ends with her marriage. A
manuscript discovered in 1971 was published under the title *The
First Four Years;* it recounts the early years of her married life
with Almanzo. *On the Way Home,* based on Laura's diary, tells
how the couple was forced to leave the farm in South Dakota
because it was unable to support all the family and relates their
trek in a covered wagon to Missouri.

Mrs. Wilder's daughter, Rose Wilder Lane, also became a
writer, and is known for her books with Missouri backgrounds.
Hill-Billy and *Cindy,* for instance, are about Ozarks people, and
her collection of short stories, *The Old Home Town,* is based on
Mansfield. The books of both women are on sale at the book and
gift shop at Rocky Ridge Farm.

Laura Ingalls Wilder's home, which is on the National Register of Historic Homes, is furnished with original pieces, many of
them made by hand by Almanzo and decorated with handwork by
Mrs. Wilder; also here is her writing desk, which traveled on the
wagon from South Dakota. The museum building houses

memorabilia and manuscripts of Mrs. Wilder and Rose Wilder
Lane. (All profits from admissions and book sales go to the repair
and upkeep of the house.)

St. Louis

St. Louis, the gateway to the West, has an impressive number of
literary associations. Joseph Pulitzer, who started his career as a
reporter for the German-language *Westliche Post* in St. Louis in
1868, became the publisher of the *St. Louis Post-Dispatch* in
1878. Kate Chopin was born in this city in 1851 of a Creole mother
and Irish father. She moved back here from Louisiana after her
husband died and began to write her stories of Creole and Cajun
life. Eugene Field (see below) was born here, and the city was
also the birthplace of the poets T. S. Eliot (1888–1965) and Sara
Teasdale (1884–1933), who is buried in Bellefontaine Cemetery on
West Florissant Avenue. The Missouri-born writer Winston
Churchill was the author of *The Crisis* (1901), a historical novel
set in St. Louis during the Civil War that deals with the conflict
over the slavery issue. William Gass, author of *In the Heart of the
Heart of the Country* and *Omensetter's Luck,* teaches at
Washington University in St. Louis. Tennessee Williams once
lived in the city. Unfortunately, the house at 2635 Locust Street
where T. S. Eliot grew up has been demolished. The apartment
building on Westminster Place where Tennessee Williams once
resided and where he set *The Glass Menagerie* is in a rotten
neighborhood. St. Louis has had its problems with urban decay.
But around the downtown riverfront area known as Laclede's
Landing there has been a lot of development and restoration, with
the Gateway Arch towering over the oldest part of the city (from
where Lewis and Clark began their expedition). A narrated tour
of the riverfront area on a Riverfront Trolley is available during
the summer.

Mark Twain knew the city well when he was working as a
riverboat pilot in the late 1850s. In *Life on the Mississippi* he
recorded his reactions when he revisited St. Louis in 1882:

The city seemed but little changed. It *was* greatly changed, but it did not seem so; because in St. Louis, as in London and Pittsburgh, you can't persuade a new thing to look new; the coal smoke turns it into an antiquity the moment you take your hand off it. The place had just about doubled its size, since I was a resident of it, and was now become a city of 400,000 inhabitants; still, in the solid business parts, it looked about as it had looked formerly.

He goes on to describe the fine new homes on the outskirts and the then new Forest Park. With tongue in cheek, he laments not having made an investment:

The first time I ever saw St. Louis, I could have bought it for six million dollars, and it was the mistake of my life that I did not do it. It was bitter now to look abroad over this domed and steepled metropolis, this solid expanse of bricks and mortar stretching away on every hand into dim, measure-defying distances, and remember that I had allowed that opportunity to go by. Why I should have allowed it to go by seems, of course, foolish and inexplicable today, at a first glance; yet there were reasons at the time to justify this course.

Twain's greatest regret was the disappearance of the steamboat traffic:

But the change of changes was on the "levee.". . . Half a dozen sound-asleep steamboats where I used to see a solid mile of wide-awake ones! This was melancholy, this was woeful. . . . The towboat and the railroad had done their work, and done it well and completely. The mighty bridge, stretching along over our heads, had done its share in the slaughter and spoliation. Remains of former steamboatmen told me, with wan satisfaction, that the bridge doesn't pay. Still, it can be no sufficient compensation to a corpse to know that the dynamite that laid him out was not of as good quality as it had been supposed to be.

Steamboating has been revived, in a sense, in the shape of two replicas of nineteenth-century Mississippi steamboats named the *Huck Finn* and the *Sam Clemens,* which take visitors on narrated sightseeing cruises on the river to view points of interest on the riverfront. The boats go under the Eads Bridge, built in 1874, the one Mark Twain refers to in the passage above. Trips leave daily,

Memorial Day through Labor Day, weekends and holidays during April, May, September, and October, 10–5, from the wharf at the foot of Washington Avenue (evening dinner cruises also available). For information, contact Streckfus Steamers, Foot of Washington Avenue, St. Louis, MO 63102; telephone 314-621-4040.

Eugene Field House and Toy Museum. 634 South Broadway (3 blocks south of Busch Stadium). Tues.–Sat. 10–4, Sun. 12–5; closed Mon. and holidays. Admission.

The Eugene Field House, built in 1845, is all that remains of what was originally a group of twelve row houses. Eugene's parents, Roswell and Frances Field, leased the second unit from the south end of Walsh's Row, and it was here that Eugene Field was born in 1850. (Roswell Field was a lawyer and became famous when he instituted the lawsuit for the freedom of the slave Dred Scott in 1847; it wasn't until 1857 that the Supreme Court finally handed down the Dred Scott decision, which declared that slaves were not citizens and therefore ineligible to bring suit in federal court.)

Eugene Field spent the first six years of his life in this house. In 1856 his mother died, and he and his brother were sent to Amherst, Massachusetts, to be raised by an aunt. A rather erratic college career (he was expelled from three colleges for his pranks and never graduated from anywhere) included some time at the University of Missouri, where he was literary editor of the campus newspaper. In May 1872 he became a reporter on the *St. Louis Journal,* and in October of that year married Julia Comstock in St. Joseph, Missouri. In 1875 he became city editor of the St. Joseph *Gazette* (his poem "Lover's Lane, Saint Jo" has made that residential street in St. Joseph famous). After his journalistic career took him first back to St. Louis and then to Kansas City and Denver, he finally settled in Chicago in 1883, where his personal, often satirical column for the Chicago *Daily News,* "Sharps and Flats," made him famous (see Chicago). He also became widely known for his popular and sentimental children's verses, some of the most famous of which are "Little Boy Blue," "The Duel" (of the calico cat and the gingham dog), "Wynken, Blynken, and Nod," and "The Sugar-Plum Tree." He died in 1895 of a stomach ailment at the age of forty-five.

The plaque on the house that reads "Here was born Eugene Field the Poet, 1850–1895" was dedicated in 1902 by no less than Mark Twain. The house was threatened with razing in 1934, but although the rest of Walsh's Row was demolished, the campaign to save this house was successful, and it was opened to the public in 1936. It is now operated by the Landmarks Association of St. Louis. The house has furniture, some of it original, of the early and mid-Victorian period; the preservation is, in the words of the brochure, "a fuller interpretation of a way of life in St. Louis 120 years ago, an enrichment of early Victoriana in the shadows of skyscrapers and expressway viaducts." Mementos and manuscripts of Eugene Field are on display, and there is an extensive collection of antique toys and dolls that appeals to adults and children alike.

MONTANA

The journals of Lewis and Clark record their trek through Montana; they mapped more than 1900 miles of previously uncharted territory in this state. The **Lewis and Clark Trail** in Montana, which includes Pompey's Pillar, where Captain Clark carved his name on July 25, 1806, is designated by historic markers and is outlined on a map available from Montana tourist offices or from the Montana Highway Commission, Helena, MT 59601.

The principal subjects of Montana literature have been the mining-boom era of the second half of the nineteenth century, the Wild West of cowboys, Indians, and outlaws, and the wide open spaces of ranch life.

The **Copper King Mansion** in **Butte** (219 West Granite Street; open daily 9–9; admission) evokes the great days of the mining boom and the "copper king wars." The novels of Myron Brinig, such as *Wide Open Town* and *The Sun Sets in the West,* are examples of writing about Montana mining. *Copper Camp,* classic stories of Butte collected by the WPA Federal Writers' Project, has recently been reissued. Virginia City (which see) is a restoration of a gold-boom town.

The West of Wild Bill Hickok, Calamity Jane, and other legendary characters who became the heroes and heroines of countless Western romances is interpreted with historical accuracy at the **Western Heritage Center** in **Billings** (2822 Montana Avenue; Tues.–Sat. 10–5, 10–7 in summer, Sun. 1–5; closed holidays; free). The **Charles M. Russell Museum and Original Studio** in **Great Falls** (1201 Fourth Avenue North) is a shrine to the great cowboy artist. *The Log of a Cowboy* (1903), a minor classic by Andy Adams, is about the cattle drives from Texas to Montana.

One of the best novels about the West by a contemporary writer is A. B. Guthrie, Jr.'s *The Big Sky,* which takes place in the pioneer Montana of the nineteenth century.

Custer Battlefield National Monument

2 miles southeast of Crow Agency; main entrance on US 212, 1 mile east of US 87, I-90. Visitor Center open daily, early June–early Sept., 7 a.m.–8:45 p.m., rest of year, 8–4:30; closed Thanksgiving, Christmas, New Year's Day. Free.

One of the most dramatic events of Western American history was the so-called Custer's Last Stand, when General George Armstrong Custer and his men were annihilated by Sioux warriors led by Chief Crazy Horse and by Sitting Bull at the Little Big Horn on June 25, 1876. The battle was the result of Sioux and Cheyenne resistance to the invasion of their land by white men seeking gold. The event has caught the imagination of scores of writers of fiction and fact. Mari Sandoz (see Gordon, Nebraska), the biographer and historian, wrote *Crazy Horse* (1942) and *The Battle of Little Big Horn* (1966), and Stanley Vestal, known for his authoritative books on the Old West, wrote *Sitting Bull. Bugles in the Afternoon* by Ernest Haycox and *Broken Lance* by Frank Gruber are both novels about Custer. A recent novel in which Custer and Little Big Horn play a role is Thomas Berger's *Little Big Man* (which became a successful film), about the allegedly only white survivor of the battle.

The site of the Last Stand is now a national monument. The Visitor Center has dioramas and exhibits interpreting the battle.

Virginia City

The first book published in Montana, and a kind of classic, was *The Vigilantes of Montana* (1866) by Thomas J. Dimsdale, a schoolteacher in Virginia City, Montana. The book is an account of the notorious Henry Plummer and his gang, who marauded through the gold strike territory in the 1860s. The **Vigilante Trail,** between Virginia City and the ghost town of **Bannack** (south of Dillon in Beaverhead National Forest), the latter of which was the first territorial capital and is now a state monument, has historical markers. It was along this trail that the gang murdered and robbed so many people that vigilantes finally got after them. Henry Plummer, the sheriff of Bannack, turned out to be the leader of the gang! He was strung up on his own gallows.

Virginia City and nearby **Nevada City** (1½ miles west of Virginia City on SR 287) have been restored. Virginia City, which was the site of Montana's second biggest gold strike and was the territorial capital from 1865 to 1875, has restorations of false-front buildings including the offices of the first Montana newspaper, a brewery, the Virginia City Opera House, and a "tonsorial parlor," plus two historical museums (open May–Sept., daily 8–6; free). Nevada City is a reconstruction, with some buildings brought from other parts of the state; these include shops, homes, offices, and a railroad museum in the depot.

These are good places to get the flavor of the Montana gold era, which has been the subject of many books, outstanding of which are Hoffman Birney's nonfiction *Vigilantes* and his novel *Ann Carmeny*.

NEBRASKA

Nebraska, a state of sturdy farmer-pioneers, has produced some outstanding literature that vividly chronicles the breaking and taming of the prairie in the nineteenth century. The greatest of the authors who drew upon this matter of Nebraska is of course Willa Cather, who although she spent only her childhood there re-created the state's past in many of her finest novels (see Red Cloud).

Bess Streeter Aldrich (1881–1954) lived in Elmwood, Cass County, and in her last years in Lincoln (both homes still stand but are private). A writer of novels of pioneers in the Middle West, she is best known for *A Lantern in Her Hand* (1928), the story of Abbie Deal, a courageous pioneer mother in Nebraska. She also wrote *Spring Came On Forever* and *The Rim of the Prairie* in addition to novels of contemporary life. A memorial marker stands in a park in Elmwood. Bronze busts of Aldrich and Cather are in the **Nebraska Hall of Fame** in the State Capitol in **Lincoln.**

Another distinguished Nebraska writer was Mari Sandoz (1896–1966), a biographer, historian, and novelist whose subject matter was pioneer life and the Old West (see Gordon). John G. Neihardt was the poet laureate of Nebraska for many years, and wrote poems and short stories about pioneers and Indians in the Old West (see Bancroft). Wright Morris was born in Central City, and although he has not lived in Nebraska for many years, many of his characters are Midwesterners. His novel *The Home Place* (1948) is about a family who returns to a Nebraska farm.

Bancroft

John G. Neihardt Center. Elm and Washington Streets (southwest corner of town). March 1–Nov. 1, Mon.–Sat. 8–5, Sun. 1–5; open rest of year by appointment. Free.

John Gneisenau Neihardt was a distinguished poet and short-story writer whose subject matter was the westward expansion and the American Indian. Born in Illinois in 1881, his family moved first to northwestern Kansas, then to Kansas City, and finally settled in Wayne, Nebraska, where he attended grade school and Nebraska Normal College. His literary talent evinced itself early: he wrote his first book, *The Divine Enchantment,* based on Vedanta philosophy, when he was sixteen (it was published before he was twenty). He taught in a country school for a couple of years, and then, when he was about twenty-one, he came to Bancroft, in northeastern Nebraska. He worked with a trader among the Omaha Indians (the Omaha reservation is just north of Bancroft) and learned their customs and traditions.

From September 1903 to January 1905 he was co-owner and editor of a weekly newspaper, the *Bancroft Blade.* After that he devoted his time fully to writing and gained national attention with his collection of short stories *The Lonesome Trail* (1907), tales of pioneers and Indians. *The River and I,* about his adventures going down the Missouri River, was published in 1910. In 1915 came *The Song of Hugh Glass,* a book-length poem that was to be the first of five that ultimately made up *A Cycle of the West,* an epic of the West that begins in 1822 and ends with the massacre at Wounded Knee in 1890 (see South Dakota for more about Hugh Glass). The other poems are *The Song of Three Friends* (1919), *The Song of the Indian Wars* (1925), *The Song of the Messiah* (1935), and *The Song of Jed Smith* (1941); they were published together in chronological sequence in 1949. Neihardt is also known for *Black Elk Speaks* (1932), which has been translated into nine languages. This prose book is a philosophical biography and a record of the sayings and stories of Black Elk, a holy man of the Oglala Sioux whom Neihardt got to know intimately. It is a treasure trove of Indian lore and an important firsthand account of the Indian way of life.

Neihardt was declared poet laureate of Nebraska in 1921. He moved to Branson, Missouri, in that year, and lived there for twenty years. He was literary editor of the *St. Louis Post-Dispatch* from 1926 to 1936, and poet in residence and lecturer in English at the University of Missouri in Columbia from 1949 to 1966. In his last years he moved back to Nebraska and lived with friends in Lincoln. He died in 1973 at the home of his daughter in Columbia, Missouri, at the age of ninety-two; at the time of his death he was working on the second volume of his autobiography.

The Neihardt Center comprises a new study center, the Neihardt Study, and the Sioux Prayer Garden. The study, originally in the backyard of Neihardt's home, is a small one-room house where Dr. Neihardt would retreat to work. Under his supervision it was restored with framed copies of manuscripts on the wall, rocking chair, kerosene lamp, potbellied stove, and old typewriter. The study is on the National Register of Historic Places.

The Sioux Prayer Garden is a circular garden symbolizing the Hoop of the World as described in *Black Elk Speaks*. Each of its four quarters has its particular color, power, and significance, and according to traditional Sioux belief, prayers are offered to each quarter so that the powers of each quarter may be given to the people. The full symbolism of the garden is explained in a leaflet given to visitors.

The new Neihardt Center is a 4000-square-foot circular building (reflecting the ideal of the Sioux Hoop of the World) and contains a memorial room with exhibits about Neihardt and a research library. A twenty-minute film called *Performing the Vision,* about Dr. Neihardt's experiences with Black Elk, is also shown. The first Sunday in August is Neihardt Day in Nebraska, and special ceremonies take place here on that day; visitors are welcome.

Gordon

The small town of Gordon, where US 20 and SR 27 intersect, in the western panhandle of Nebraska, is in the sandhills country about which the regional writer Mari Sandoz (1896–1966) wrote extensively and eloquently. Born in Sheridan County, Nebraska, the daughter of a Swiss immigrant, Jules Sandoz, she grew up on a homestead in this area, and although she spent much of her adult life in the East, particularly in New York, she wrote mainly about the West.

As a young woman she worked for the Nebraska State Historical Society in Lincoln, and wrote many short stories during this period. She first gained wide attention in 1935 with the publication of *Old Jules,* a biography of her father, which won the *Atlantic Monthly* prize. A realistic and brutally unsentimental account of an eventful life that included four marriages, six children, immigration from Switzerland, battles with cattlemen, lawsuits, and struggle for survival on the frontier, it was hailed by critics; Stephen Vincent Benét said it was "the best and most honest picture of its kind since Hamlin Garland's *A Son of the Middle Border."* Some of her other better-known books are the novel *Slogum House* (1937), the nonfiction *Love Song to the Plains* (1961), and her narratives about the Indians, *Crazy Horse* (1942) and *Cheyenne Autumn* (1953). She was no doubt inspired to write these last two by the proximity of historic Fort Robinson, now **Fort Robinson State Park and Museum** (4 miles west of the town of Crawford, which is west of Gordon; museum open Apr.–Nov., daily 8–5, longer hours in summer; free). This was the headquarters of the United States Army for their battles with the Sioux and Cheyenne, where Cheyenne were imprisoned and Crazy Horse, in 1877, was killed. The town of Crawford has a **Crazy Horse Museum** in the city park (open weekends in summer; free).

In Gordon the **Chamberlin Furniture Store** (122 North Main Street) has a **Mari Sandoz Room** (open year round; free) with displays of memorabilia, awards, and scrapbooks. About twenty-one miles south on SR 27 (across the Niobrara River), in a rest area park at the site of the old Sandoz homestead, is a **look-in museum** set up to duplicate the author's Greenwich Village apartment, in which she did most of her writing in later life. Nearby are her grave and some of the orchards Old Jules began, still owned by a Sandoz family member. Detailed tour maps of the area are available at Chamberlin Furniture.

The **Mari Sandoz Heritage Society** has been established at Chadron State College in **Chadron** (47 miles west of Gordon via US 20). The **Mari Sandoz Heritage Room** in the library of the college is open by appointment only; it contains books, historical material, oral history tapes of pioneer Nebraskans, and other research sources. The society sponsors a biennial Sandoz Country Tour in June. For information write Mari Sandoz Heritage Society, Chadron State College, Chadron, NE 69337.

Red Cloud

Willa Cather was born in Virginia on December 7, 1873. In the spring of 1883, when Willa was nine, her father, Charles Cather, decided to sell his Virginia property and join his father, brother, and a group of other Virginians in Nebraska. When the family first came west they lived on a farm northwest of the town of Red Cloud, on the high flat plains. The bleak and empty landscape was a shocking contrast to the Shenandoah Valley Willa had left, and at first she was terribly homesick. Gradually, however, she came to know and love the open prairie, which had just begun to be broken by the plows of the settlers. She lived on her grandfather's homestead on what was called the Divide for eighteen months, and it is this landscape that figures so importantly in her Nebraska books, especially *O Pioneers!* and *My Ántonia*. She met for the first time people who did not speak English, the Swedish, Danish, Norwegian, and Bohemian settlers who were transformed into central characters in her novels.

In September 1884 Willa's father moved his family once more, but only into the town of Red Cloud, where he set up a business selling insurance and making farm loans. Red Cloud in 1884 had existed for only fourteen years, having been founded by Captain Silas Garber in 1870 (he is the prototype for Captain Forrester in *A Lost Lady*). When the Cather family moved into the one-and-a-half-story house at the corner of Cedar and Third Streets, Red Cloud (whimsically named after a Sioux chief) was a bustling town of about 2500 people. Eight trains of the Burlington Railroad (on which Jim Burden in *My Ántonia* arrives) went through town daily. Willa went to grade school and high school here, and all through her childhood and adolescence absorbed impressions of the people and life in the town and the surrounding farms that became the rich material of her novels. She lived in Red Cloud until 1890, when she left to attend the University of Nebraska in Lincoln.

Red Cloud is thoroughly imbued with the spirit of Willa Cather, as her books are imbued with the spirit of Red Cloud. It is called Hanover in *O Pioneers!,* Moonstone in *The Song of the Lark* (although the novel is set in Colorado, the descriptions of the town match Red Cloud), Black Hawk in *My Ántonia,* Frankfort in *One of Ours,* Sweet Water in *A Lost Lady,* and Haverford in *Lucy Gayheart*; it is also the setting for the stories in *Obscure Destinies.* The Willa Cather Pioneer Memorial is a local organization that has done an excellent and scholarly job of identifying and preserving buildings and sites in and around Red Cloud. Two tours are available: the town tour (modest fee per adult; includes entrance to five buildings) and the "Catherland" tour (self-guided; written guides and map provided). An independent walking tour can also be taken, following the map available at the museum.

Both tours begin at the **Willa Cather Pioneer Memorial Museum and Archives,** on Webster Street, two doors south of Fourth Avenue (May 1–Oct. 1, daily 10:30–5; rest of year, 1–5 weekends, and by appointment; admission). The museum occupies the former Farmers' and Merchants' Bank Building, erected in 1899 by Silas Garber, mentioned above as the model for Captain Forrester in *A Lost Lady.* The museum features a slide show about Willa Cather and Red Cloud and has many original Cather letters and manuscripts, first editions, and other mementos.

Of greatest interest in the town is the **Cather Childhood Home,** on the southwest corner of Cedar and Third Streets (separate admission without tour). This story-and-a-half white frame house, now completely restored, was the best Charles Cather could find at the time he moved his family into Red Cloud. Cather writes affectionately about it in her story "The Best Years," where she describes her upstairs room with its slanting ceiling, "where there were no older people poking about to spoil things." This is also the house that Thea Kronborg lives in in *The Song of the Lark,* and also appears in the story "Old Mrs. Harris." The walls of her cozy room still have the very wallpaper, now faded, of red and brown roses that Willa earned by working in **Cook's drugstore** (the second brick building from the corner of Fourth Avenue, across the street from the Opera House, where Willa attended her high school graduation ceremonies). The Cather Childhood Home is a National Historic Landmark.

The tour of Red Cloud also takes in, among many landmarks associated with Cather and her works, the old **Burlington Depot** (south end of Seward Street); the **Miner Home** (at Seward Street and Third Avenue), the original of the **Harling house** where Ántonia worked in *My Ántonia;* the **St. Juliana Catholic Church** (south of Division Street, on Third Street and Seward Street), where Ántonia was married; and the **Grace Episcopal Church** (Cedar Street and Sixth Avenue), which Cather joined in 1922. All the Cather sites in Red Cloud are marked by signs, as are the locations in the Catherland tour around the western part of Webster County.

This auto tour, which is about fifty miles, covers many sites familiar to readers of Cather's works. Starting in Red Cloud and passing the cottonwood grove east of town that served as the setting for *A Lost Lady,* you drive south to the Republican River; then you head west and north, coming upon the **Dane Church** on the Bladen Road, the site of the old Cather homestead (the Burden homestead of *My Ántonia*), and then entering the section known as the Divide. Three miles east of Bladen and a mile and a half south is the **Cloverton cemetery,** where John and Anna Pavelka, the originals of John Cuzak and Ántonia Shimerda, are buried, and just one mile south on the right-hand side of the road is the **Pavelka farmhouse** with its fruit cave, which appears in *My*

Ántonia; the Cather Pioneer Memorial has acquired the property and is restoring it.

Five miles south of Red Cloud is the **Willa Cather Memorial Prairie,** a 610-acre section of virgin prairie set aside by the Nature Conservancy in honor of Willa Cather. This tract of native grassland, with its tall shaggy grass and wildflowers, is an example of what Cather once called ''the floor of the sky,'' and reflects what most of this part of Nebraska looked like when the pioneers Cather wrote about first arrived.

NEVADA

Nevada has its share of appearances as the locale for Western novels, of course. Zane Grey (inevitably) wrote a book set here, simply titled *Nevada*. Walter Van Tilburg Clark's fine novel *The Ox-Bow Incident,* called by some the best Western ever written, is laid in the Nevada of the 1880s. The great subject matter of Nevada, though, is the discovery of the Comstock Lode, the fabulous vein of silver that brought in thousands of people where there had been hardly any before and created dozens of boom towns. *Artemus Ward, His Travels* (1865) includes amusing sketches of the early great days in Carson City and Virginia City by the famous humorist (Charles Farrar Browne), who was a great influence on Mark Twain (he met Twain in Virginia City and later helped him get published in the East). Fred H. Hart, a Nevada frontier journalist and humorist who flourished in the 1870s, was the author of *The Sazerac Lying Club* (1878), a collection of tall tales and funny sketches. Vardis Fisher's novel *City of Illusion* is but one of many more recent books about the bonanza in Washoe (as the territory was then called). But the name forever associated with Virginia City and Nevada is, of course, Mark Twain, whose professional writing career can be said to have truly begun here.

Carson City

When the Civil War halted Mississippi riverboat traffic, Samuel Clemens found himself out of work as a pilot. He joined the Confederate army in Missouri as a second lieutenant, but, as he relates in his *Autobiography*, "I resigned after two weeks' service in the field, explaining that I was 'incapacitated by fatigue' through persistent retreating." Luckily, his older brother Orion had obtained the post of secretary to the governor of the territory of Nevada, and offered Sam a position as his assistant. In 1861 Sam accompanied Orion on the trip by overland stage to the West, described hilariously in *Roughing It*. He writes of his stay in Carson City in *Roughing It* and in his *Autobiography*. After living at a boardinghouse with his brother for a time, Sam decided to try his luck at mining, and roamed around the countryside speculating in mine shares and looking for a silver claim. He mined with Calvin H. Higbie at **Aurora** (then called Esmeralda), now a ghost town (35 miles southwest of Hawthorne off SR 31), but went off to nurse a sick friend and returned too late to save their possible fortune from claim jumpers. He finally gave up trying to become rich as a miner (at least temporarily—he tried again in California) and went to Virginia City to work on the *Territorial Enterprise,* to which he had previously contributed some letters signed "Josh." He was sent back to Carson City to report the legislative session, and it was at this time that he began signing his reports with the name Mark Twain ("two fathoms" in riverboat jargon).

Orion did well as territorial secretary, and because of Governor Nye's frequent absences, he was often the acting governor. Twain writes in his *Autobiography* of the pleasure Orion's wife took in being a "governor's wife":

> No one on this planet ever enjoyed a distinction more than she enjoyed that one. Her delight in being the head of society was so frank that it disarmed criticism and even envy. Being the Governor's wife and head of society, she looked for a proper kind of

house to live in—a house commensurate with these dignities—
and she easily persuaded Orion to build that house. Orion could
be persuaded to do anything. He built and furnished the house
at a cost of twelve thousand dollars and there was no other
house in that capital that could approach this property for style
and cost.

This house, built in 1863, still stands in Carson City, at **502 North
Division Street** (at Spear Street). It had a shiplap exterior (boards
fitted together) and was later stuccoed. Sam stayed with his
brother here while he was in Carson City. It is privately owned
and not open to the public, but it is one of the features on the
historic tour of Carson City, which includes many other old mansions built during the silver boom years. For a map and further
information contact the Chamber of Commerce, 1190 South Carson Street, Carson City, NV 89701.

East of Carson City is **Lake Tahoe.** Twain has a lovely description of an idyllic interlude he spent at the lake in *Roughing It.*

The **Bowers Mansion** (10 miles north on US 395; mid-May–
Oct., daily 11–12:30, 1:30–4:30; small admission) is an exception-
ally ornate mansion built by a Comstock Lode millionaire who
later went broke; his widow wound up telling fortunes to make a
meager living.

Virginia City

The mining mania had seized Sam Clemens, as it had practically
everyone else in the Nevada Territory of the early 1860s (except,
apparently, his brother Orion). But Clemens, still in his twenties,
was dismally unsuccessful at making his fortune in silver, as he
graphically relates in *Roughing It.* While in the mining camps he
had written satirical letters to the *Virginia City Territorial Enterprise,* signed ''Josh,'' and to his surprise, they were published.
Eventually, Sam was offered a regular job as a reporter by the
editor of the paper, Joe Goodman, and Sam, by this time completely discouraged by his singular failure to become a millionaire, accepted the twenty-five-dollar-a-week job. He showed

up in Virginia City in September 1862, having walked and hitch-hiked from Carson City.

Virginia City, or just Virginia, as it was then called, was the Queen of the Comstock Lode, a boom town with hotels, stores, saloons, brothels, even churches—and not one but several news-papers. Sam Clemens entered into the rough-and-tumble life of Virginia with zest. He was taken in hand by Dan De Quille (Wil-liam Wright), the city editor, called Local or Localitems, who became his mentor and good friend. De Quille was himself the author of *History of the Big Bonanza*. Sent to Carson City to cover the second Territorial Legislature, Sam began signing his articles Mark Twain, and of course, the nom de plume stuck. He developed quickly into a brash reporter, and he found plenty to report about. As he writes in *Roughing It*:

> . . . As I grew better acquainted with the business and learned the run of sources of information I ceased to require the aid of fancy to any large extent, and became able to fill my columns without diverging noticeably from the domain of fact.
>
> I struck up friendships with the reporters of the other jour-nals, and we swapped "regulars" with each other and thus economized work. "Regulars" are permanent sources of news, like courts, bullion returns, "clean-ups" at quartz mills, and inquests. Inasmuch as everybody went armed, we had an in-quest about every day, and so this department was naturally set down among the "regulars." We had lively papers in those days.

In May of 1864 Mark Twain insulted James L. Laird, the owner of the rival *Union,* in print; a furious exchange of letters in the two papers ensued, and finally a challenge to a duel was issued impetuously by Twain. In his *Autobiography* he tells a story about how Laird backed out when he was misinformed that Twain was a dead shot (although in truth, Twain writes, he liter-ally could not hit a barn door). But Paul Fatout, in *Mark Twain in Virginia City,* is probably correct when he states that Mark Twain (who was, to say the least, prone to exaggeration) and his friend and second, Steve Gillis, got out of town and out of Nevada altogether to avoid being prosecuted under a new antidueling law. And so he left for San Francisco, his greatest acquisitions from

Washoe (as this part of Nevada was sometimes called) not silver or gold but professional writing experience and a name.

In 1952 the journalist Lucius Beebe revived the *Territorial Enterprise*. His book *Comstock Commotion: The Story of The Territorial Enterprise* was published in 1954, and in collaboration with Charles Clegg, who edited the paper, he published *Legends of the Comstock Lode,* tales about the silver bonanza.

Much in Virginia City has been restored to the condition it was in during the 1860s. The **Visitors' Bureau** on C Street shows a fifteen-minute film, *The Story of Virginia* (see this first). Old ornate mansions of the silver kings can be toured and historic churches and cemeteries visited. The **Ophir open pit,** the site of the original 1859 discovery of the Comstock Lode, is at the west end of Sutton Avenue. Old-time saloons and the Piper Opera House, with elaborate Victorian trappings, also reflect the exuberant life of the town. There are also tours of the mines and the Sutro Tunnel, which drained water from the mines.

The **Mark Twain Museum of Memories** (C Street at Taylor), operated by the Virginia City Historical Society, has Comstock Lode memorabilia, nickelodeons, player pianos, old posters, toy trains, and Mark Twain's rolltop desk at which (supposedly) he wrote for the paper. A half block north on C Street is the office of the **Territorial Enterprise,** now also a museum.

Virginia City is only fifteen minutes from Carson City. There are restaurants and overnight accommodations in Virginia City. For further information, go to the Visitors' Bureau on C Street or write Storey County Chamber of Commerce, P.O. Box 464, Virginia City, NV 89440.

NORTH DAKOTA

The first written account of North Dakota appears in the journals of Lewis and Clark. Meriwether Lewis and William Clark spent the winter of 1804–05 at a place they called Fort Mandan, among the Mandan Indians. It was here that they met the French trapper Charbonneau, who joined them on their westward journey in the spring, and Charbonneau's young pregnant wife Sacajawea, a Shoshoni who had been captured earlier by the Minnetarees and eventually ended up in Charbonneau's company. She, of course, became the guide and interpreter for the expedition (a statue of Sacajawea is at the state capitol in Bismarck). **Fort Mandan Historic Site** (40 miles north of Bismark on US 83, then west of Washburn) is a reconstruction of the log fort Lewis and Clark erected. The **Lewis and Clark Trail Museum** in **Alexander** (Memorial Day–Labor Day, Mon.–Sat. 9–6, Sun. 1–6; admission) has a diorama of Fort Mandan in addition to exhibits on pioneer life. Bernard DeVoto's *The Course of Empire* deals with the Lewis and Clark expedition, as does Emerson Hough's *The Magnificent Adventure*.

The wars with the Dakota Sioux have been the subject matter of numerous books. Paul I. Wellman's *Death on the Prairie* (1934) is a history of the Dakota Sioux. It was from **Fort Abraham Lincoln,** now a state park (3 miles south of Mandan on county road 1806) that General Custer started out for his fateful meeting with the Sioux at the Little Big Horn in Montana in 1876. His widow, Elizabeth Custer, in her book *Boots and Saddles: or Life in Dakota with General Custer,* mainly an apologia for her husband, describes her life at this outpost. The park (open daily June–Aug. 8–8; free) has a museum, the foundations of the original fort, reconstructed blockhouses, and a partially restored Mandan village of earth lodges. (See Custer Battlefield, Montana, for more about Custer.)

An excellent recent novel laid in North Dakota is Larry Woiwode's *Beyond the Bedroom Wall* (1975), a chronicle about a midwestern family.

Medora

Theodore Roosevelt National Memorial Park. Divided into 3 units: South Unit entrance at Medora; Visitor Center, daily, June 15–Labor Day 8–8, rest of year 8–4:30. Elkhorn Ranch Site has difficult access; information at Park Headquarters in Medora. North Unit entrance on US 85, south of Watford City. Park open all year; closed Thanksgiving, Christmas, New Year's Day. Admission.

Theodore Roosevelt qualifies as a man of letters as much as a politician. Despite his time-consuming public life he wrote voluminously, publishing, among many books, the four-volume history *The Winning of the West* and *The Strenuous Life: Essays and Addresses.*

In September 1883 Roosevelt, then a twenty-five-year-old New York assemblyman, came out to the badlands of North Dakota to hunt buffalo. He became interested in the cattle business and became a partner in the Maltese Cross Ranch. He returned to New York after the hunt, but in February 1884 his young wife and his mother died on the same day. Despondent, he returned to the Dakota ranch to recover from his grief. Medora at the time was a cattle-boom town, the gathering place for ranchers whose cattle grazed on the grasses of the unfenced prairie. Roosevelt continued as a partner in the Maltese Cross Ranch and also established the Elkhorn Ranch as his own cattle-raising operation. The freedom of the outdoor life appealed to him tremendously, and he wrote that "there are few sensations I prefer to that of galloping over these rolling limitless prairies, or winding my way among the barren, fantastic and grimly picturesque deserts of the so-called Badlands.''

Disaster struck in 1886. An unusually hot summer dried up much of the grassland, and the severe winter that followed, accompanied by heavy snows, buried the grass that was left. Thousands of cattle froze to death or died of starvation. Many cattlemen lost their herds, and Roosevelt's cattle were substantially reduced in number. By that time, however, he had returned to New York to run for mayor of New York City, but he was defeated that November. A month later he married his second wife, and after this time made only brief visits to North Dakota. He sold all his ranch holdings in 1898. But the adventure of being a cowboy in one of the last vestiges of the Wild West stayed with him and influenced his thinking on conservation.

At the **Visitor Center** in Medora is the restored **Maltese Cross Cabin,** relocated from its original site, which was used by Roosevelt on his visits here. In the park, which includes some of the acreage in Roosevelt's ranches, can be seen buffalo, antelope, prairie dogs, and other wildlife in the natural rugged landscape carved by the Little Missouri River. Information about the ecology, as well as about camping and other facilities, is available at park headquarters.

In Medora are a number of tourist attractions. The **Rough Riders Hotel** (still in operation), built in 1884, gave Roosevelt the name for his Spanish-American War regiment (a caricature statue of ''Teddy'' stands rather too cutely outside). Other historic buildings in the town are the **Joe Ferris Store,** dating from 1885 and once owned by one of Roosevelt's ranching partners, and **St. Mary's Catholic Church** (1885). There is also a museum with historical exhibits.

Most interesting is the **Chateau de Mores State Historic Site** (1 mile west of town off I-94; open daily 8–5, but closed in bad weather; small admission). The twenty-six-room frame residence was built by the Marquis de Mores, a young French nobleman who came here in 1883 to start a meat-packing business. (He named the town after his wife, Medora von Hoffman, daughter of a wealthy New York banker; she was an excellent horsewoman, ahead of her time in wearing trousers instead of a skirt for riding.) His idea was to slaughter the cattle at the source and then ship the dressed beef to the consumer. This scheme would, he thought, supersede the traditional system of shipping the live cattle by railroad to the slaughterhouses in Chicago and other centers. He built a packing plant (only the chimney survives) and had special refrigerator railroad cars. At first the plan was a success, and the town of Medora prospered. But problems of feeding the cattle and the catastrophic winter of 1886–87 soon turned the boom to a bust, and the marquis left the Dakota Territory to go on to other adventurous schemes (he was killed in a battle in the Sahara in 1896). The chateau has been restored and is filled with French furniture, Oriental carpets, and fine china brought over by the marquis. Donald Dresden's *Marquis de Mores: Emperor of the Badlands* tells the story of this unique character. A recent novel that deals with the cattle wars of the Dakotas and Wyoming and has characters loosely based on Roosevelt and the Marquis de Mores is *The Bad Lands* (1978) by Oakley Hall.

During the summer, the **Medora Musical,** with a professional cast, is presented nightly in the Gold Seal Amphitheater (admission; tickets at Rough Rider Hotel).

OHIO

One of the earliest accounts of life in Ohio, which in the late eighteenth and early nineteenth centuries was the western frontier of the United States, was *Recollections of the Last Ten Years* (1826) by Timothy Flint, a minister who had settled in Ohio.

In the early days of the Ohio territory, Cincinnati was a lively literary center, and the leading writers of the 1830s and 1840s there were James Hall, Daniel Drake, and William Davis Gallagher. Hall began his writing career in Illinois (see Illinois introduction) but later became a banker in Cincinnati while continuing to produce many books on the West (the "West" being at the time the Northwest Territory), including *The Romance of Western History* and the monumental *History of the Indian Tribes of North America*. Drake was a physician who wrote an important book on the diseases of the region, but was also the author of volumes on history, culture, and geography. As the president of the School of Literature and the Arts, a Cincinnati literary club, he was the dean of the intelligentsia and literati of Cincinnati for decades. Gallagher, called William "Dignity" Gallagher because though poor he had a haughty demeanor, was a poet and journalist who edited *Selections from the Poetical Literature of the West* (1840), which contained the work of the best poets of the western territories, including several of his own poems, the best known of which is "Miami Woods," a mystical-lyrical tribute to the beauty of the Ohio Valley (the Great and Little Miami Rivers flow into the Ohio near Cincinnati).

In later years, Ohio produced a large number of major writers, but most of them left the state at the beginning of their careers. Hence, no distinctively regional literature developed, a fact that may be attributed to Ohio's rapid growth and industrialization.

Ambrose Bierce was born in Ohio in 1842; his writing, however, evinces no traces of his birthplace. William Dean Howells, on the other hand, found material in his youth in Ohio for autobiographical and fictional works. Born in Martins Ferry in 1837, he was taken to Hamilton when he was three, and later to Dayton, where his father ran a newspaper (eventually a financial failure) and where young Howells got his first experience in journalism. He later moved to Columbus and worked on the *Ohio State Journal* before he made his famous trip to Boston in 1860, after writing a campaign biography of Lincoln. *Years of My Youth* is an account of his early years in Ohio, and *A Boy's Town* is an autobiographical novel set in Hamilton. *My Year in a Log Cabin* (also autobiographical) and the novels *New Leaf Mills* and *The Leatherwood God* also have Ohio settings. Martins Ferry is also known as the home of Betty Zane in her later life. She was seventeen years old when she became the heroine of Fort Henry, across the river in Wheeling, West Virginia, by bringing American soldiers needed gunpowder during an important Revolutionary War battle in 1777. She lived to the age of sixty-three and is buried in Walnut Grove Cemetery in Martins Ferry, where there is a Betty Zane monument, a statue depicting the young girl carrying the gunpowder. Zane Grey (born in Zanesville; see museum entry under Norwich) wrote a novel called *Betty Zane* about his ancestor.

The most famous book about Ohio is doubtless Sherwood Anderson's *Winesburg, Ohio;* Anderson modeled Winesburg on the town of Clyde (which see), where he grew up. Other important writers born in Ohio are Paul Laurence Dunbar (see Dayton); Hart Crane (born in Garretsville, went to high school in Cleveland, lived awhile in Akron, and left as soon as he could); and James Thurber, who was born in Columbus and attended Ohio State University there. The play *The Male Animal,* written by him and Elliott Nugent, takes place at a large midwestern university like Ohio State. The James Thurber Reading Room in the Division of Special Collections of the university library houses the largest collection of Thurber works, including books, manuscripts, letters, and drawings.

The *Kenyon Review,* the literary quarterly, was founded at Kenyon College in Gambier in 1939. Its first editor was John

Crowe Ransom, and its original advisory board included Allen Tate, Robert Penn Warren, and Mark Van Doren.

Ohio has been the locale of several well-known fictional works. Theodore Dreiser's *Jennie Gerhardt* is set in Columbus and Cleveland. Conrad Richter's trilogy *The Trees, The Fields,* and *The Town,* the last of which won the 1951 Pulitzer Prize for fiction, is about the settling of the Ohio wilderness after the Revolutionary War. Louis Bromfield, who lived on a farm in Ohio, set many of his books in the state (see Lucas).

Cincinnati

Stowe House State Memorial. 2950 Gilbert Avenue at Foraker Avenue. June–Sept., Wed., Sun., and holidays, 10–12, 1–5. Admission.

Charles Dickens visited Cincinnati in 1842 and wrote in his *American Notes* that it "is a beautiful city; cheerful, thriving, and animated. I have not often seen a place that commends itself so favourably and pleasantly to a stranger at the first glance as this does. . . ." It was, in fact, one of the few American cities he liked when he toured the country. Cincinnati was already, in the first half of the nineteenth century, a lively and busy city, due largely to its strategic location on the Ohio River. It was to Cincinnati that Lyman Beecher removed in 1832, when he was appointed president of the new Lane Theological Seminary. His daughters Catharine and Harriet (then twenty-one) came with him. Harriet was strongly influenced by her elder sister Catharine. She had assisted her as a student teacher at the Hartford Female Seminary, and when they moved to Cincinnati, Harriet continued teaching at a new school Catharine had established, the Western Female Institute. Harriet also began writing, and contributed to the *Western Monthly Magazine* and other periodicals.

On January 6, 1836, she married Calvin E. Stowe, a young widower who was a professor in her father's seminary and who was to become a distinguished biblical scholar. Existence was hard for the Stowes. Her husband's precarious health, their lack of money, and seven children (all but the last born in Cincinnati) made Mrs. Stowe's life one of privation, anxiety, and overwork. Nevertheless, she continued to write and in 1843 published her first work of fiction, *The Mayflower*.

Because of its proximity to the slave state of Kentucky, just across the river, Cincinnati before the Civil War was a key stop on the Underground Railroad. Loyalties were divided in the city, since Cincinnati's strong economic ties to the South made pro-slavery sentiment strong among much of the population, but there was also a great deal of abolitionist activity, particularly among the transplanted New Englanders. (During the Civil War, the city was loyal to the Union side.) At first, Harriet, although she thought slavery an evil, was not a radical abolitionist. But it was while living in Cincinnati with her husband and family that Harriet Beecher Stowe first conceived the idea of writing *Uncle Tom's Cabin*. She visited a plantation across the river in Kentucky and observed slavery at first hand. She had heard the story of Eliza at the house of John Rankin in Ripley (which see), a town east of Cincinnati on the Ohio River, and her contacts with others involved in the antislavery movement provided her with other material that was ultimately incorporated into the novel. The famous book itself was written in Brunswick, Maine, where the Stowes moved in 1850 when Calvin was appointed professor at Bowdoin College.

The Stowe House is really Lyman Beecher's house, built for him as the residence of the president of Lane Seminary. Harriet lived here before her marriage and visited frequently afterward. It is now a museum of black history, particularly in Ohio, with displays on the history of the abolitionist movement as well as some exhibits on Mrs. Stowe.

Clyde

Clyde is the northern Ohio town where Sherwood Anderson grew up (he was born in Camden, Ohio) and which he transformed into Winesburg, Ohio. The fourth of seven children, Anderson did not have an easy childhood. His father was a harness maker by trade, and a drinking man by habit. He is the "Windy" of *Windy McPherson's Son* (1916), Anderson's first novel. Anderson had little formal schooling because he had to go to work early to help support the family; he acquired the nickname "Jobby" because he was always looking for odd jobs. He worked on farms, in shops, and in livery and racing stables, the last appearing frequently in his short stories. His difficult boyhood, with its emotional and financial insecurity, became one of the major themes of his writing. His autobiographical volumes *A Story Teller's Story* (1924), *Tar: A Midwest Childhood* (1926), and *Sherwood Anderson's Memoirs* (published posthumously in 1942) all tell of his formative years in Clyde. When Anderson was nineteen his mother died at the age of forty-five of tuberculosis aggravated by overwork and exhaustion. The family broke up and Anderson made the first of several moves in his life, to Chicago.

When *Winesburg, Ohio* was published in 1919, he gained worldwide attention. His psychological insights into his characters trapped by the conventionality and spiritual poverty of small-town life and his depiction of the adolescent rebellion of George Willard against the confinement of the town won him great acclaim—but not in Clyde. Like Edgar Lee Masters, Sinclair Lewis, and Thomas Wolfe, he was a prophet not without honor, save in his own country. There he was reviled as being the author of a "dirty book" who had maliciously depicted the townspeople in a bad light, although the specific characters in the book were apparently all totally imaginary creations. The local librarian burned the book when it first came out, and resentment died hard in the town. Now, however, all is either forgiven or forgotten, and Clyde pays a modest tribute to Anderson with a small exhibit of photos and memorabilia in the **Clyde Museum** in the basement of the Public Library at 222 West Buckeye Street (library open daily 10–8:30, Sat. 10–5:30; museum open Wed. evenings 5:30–8:30, and on request to a library staff member). The Anderson family's home was at 120 Spring Avenue, now a private residence.

Dayton

Paul Laurence Dunbar House State Memorial. 219 North Summit Street. June–Sept., Wed.–Sat. 10–5, Sun. 1–5; closed rest of year. Small admission.

Paul Laurence Dunbar was born in Dayton in 1872, the only child of parents who had escaped slavery in Kentucky. He went to the public schools of Dayton and graduated from Steele High School, where although he was the only black student he was very popular and was editor of the school newspaper. He began writing at an early age, and had poems published in local newspapers. He sold his first short story when he was nineteen, but the only job he could find was running an elevator. He continued to write, however, despite poverty and hardship, and published his first volume of poetry at his own expense (*Oak and Ivy,* 1893). His second book of verse, *Majors and Minors* (1895) came to the attention of William Dean Howells, who wrote a full-page admiring review of his work for *Harper's Weekly.* The recognition that resulted enabled him to get a real publisher for his next volume, *Lyrics of Lowly Life* (1896), with an introduction written by Howells. He quickly became one of America's most popular poets. He was in demand as a lecturer, toured England, was appointed to a position at the Library of Congress, and married Alice Ruth Moore, herself a writer, in 1898.

Dunbar's health was frail, however. He spent a winter in Colorado in an effort to arrest the tuberculosis that was wasting him away, but when he returned east, he was still ill. He separated from his wife around this time, too. In 1903 he returned to Dayton, to this house, where his mother lived. He died here in 1906 at the age of thirty-three.

Dunbar was called the "poet laureate of the Negro race" by Booker T. Washington. Although Dunbar himself preferred his verse written in traditional meter and style, he was most successful in his dialect poems and stories. His house is now a memorial to one of the earliest and most successful of black American writers.

Lucas

Malabar Farm State Park. On Pleasant Valley Road, just west of SR 603, 12 miles southeast of Mansfield. Farm open daily 9–5. Guided tours of Louis Bromfield's home daily 9–5; house closed Thanksgiving, Christmas, and Sundays in Dec.–Feb. Admission.

Louis Bromfield, born in 1898 in Mansfield, Ohio, gained fame with the publication of his first novel, *The Green Bay Tree,* in 1925. His 1926 novel *Early Autumn* won the Pulitzer Prize. In 1927 he moved to France with his wife and daughter and remained there until the outbreak of World War II, when he returned to the United States with his family. He came back to Ohio, where he purchased four neglected farms near Mansfield; he named his newly acquired 640-acre property Malabar, after the Malabar coastal region of India where his successful 1937 novel *The Rains Came* is set.

As a child Bromfield had observed his grandfather's efforts to restore old farms and had acquired a love of the land. He had attended the Cornell University School of Agriculture as a youth and now tried to apply his knowledge, using the "horse sense farming principles" of his grandfather and the methods of the French farmers he had observed. His almost mystical reverence for the land and the cycle of life led him to initiate a program of soil, water, forest, and wildlife conservation in a framework of a kind of "capitalist" operation with well-paid tenant farmers, who succeeded in combating erosion with "grass farming," which helped rejuvenate and preserve the soil. Other improvements included using ponds for fire protection and hedges instead of wire for barriers for livestock; these multiflora rose "fences" also offered refuge for birds.

His home started with a small house he found on the farm. He kept adding on to this base, until he had a house of thirty-two rooms. Designed by Bromfield himself and the architect Louis Lamoreux, the "Big House" is a blend of Ohio styles deliberately made to look as if it had been added onto over the years. No expense was spared in decorating the sprawling house. Bromfield's study had an enormous desk with twenty-eight drawers, and its walls were lined with bookcases. The main hall has a floating double staircase. In the living room a mirrored wall with gilt stars and a golden eagle mounted on top surrounds the mantel. Artwork and antiques are everywhere. The house still contains original furnishings.

Bromfield paid for the house—and, in fact, for the operation of the farm, which was not self-supporting—from the sales of his many popular books and especially from the sale of the movie rights and the film scripts he wrote. Although the literary quality of his work may have deteriorated in the 1940s, its salability increased: *Mrs. Parkington,* for instance, was sold to MGM for a very large sum. With his involvement in films came friendships with movie stars, and many were guests at Malabar: James Cagney, Kay Francis, and numerous others. Humphrey Bogart and Lauren Bacall were married in the rose garden and spent their honeymoon here.

Bromfield's later writings went beyond his popular novels. He also wrote four books about his farm and his agricultural theories: *Pleasant Valley* (1945), *Malabar Farm* (1948), *Out of the Earth* (1950), and *From My Experience* (1955). By the time of the last book, though, Bromfield's popularity had waned, the money from book and movie sales had stopped coming in, and he could no longer pump money into the farm. When he died in March 1956, it seemed as if Malabar Farm was fated to be cut up by real estate developers. A foundation was formed to preserve the farm intact, and in 1972 operation of Malabar Farm was assumed by the state of Ohio. At present 280 acres of land are under cultivation and a dairy herd is also being built up. In addition to a guided tour of the house, a tractor-drawn wagon tour of the farm, with explanations of the agricultural methods, is given April through October on Sundays at 2:30 for a small extra fee.

Nearby, down Pleasant Valley Road, is the Malabar Inn, built in 1820. It is the "Old Bailey Place" referred to by Bromfield in his Malabar Farm writings. Now state-owned, it operates as a restaurant (open May–October).

Norwich

The National Road–Zane Grey Museum. 8850 East Pike, on US 40, Norwich exit of I-70, 10 miles east of Zanesville. Mon.–Sat. 9:30–5, Sun. and holidays 11–5; closed Thanksgiving, Christmas, New Year's Day. Admission.

Zane Grey was born in Zanesville in 1872. His great-grandfather, Ebenezer Zane, had cut the first public trace through the Ohio wilderness, and Zanesville rose on his land. Grey's birthplace is at 705 Convers Avenue in Zanesville (private residence, not open to the public). Zane Grey is, of course, known for his prolific output of Westerns, but his first novel was *Betty Zane,* about the Revolutionary War heroine of Fort Henry (see Ohio introduction). He set two other historical novels in the Ohio Valley, which together with *Betty Zane* form a trilogy: *Spirit of the Border* and *The Last Trail.*

There used to be a small Zane Grey exhibit in a bank building in Zanesville, but when the National Road–Zane Grey Museum opened in 1973, the displays were transferred and augmented. The Ohio Historical Society, which operates the museum, was the recipient of gifts from Grey's family, including manuscripts, first editions, trophies, and personal mementos, many of which are on exhibit. The museum also has a reconstruction of Grey's study in Altadena, California, where he did much of his writing in his later years. A life-size model of the author depicts him working on a manuscript.

The "National Road" part of the museum illustrates the history of the important road that stretched from Cumberland, Maryland, to Vandalia, Illinois, and that was the key link between East and West in the early nineteenth century, before the coming of the railroad. Historic vehicles, different types of paving materials, and re-creations of scenes of life along the road in dioramas constitute this carefully researched and well-presented exhibit. In 1925 what had once been the National Road became US 40, alongside of which the museum stands.

Oxford

McGuffey Museum of Miami University. Spring and Oak Streets, on campus of Miami University. Tues. 2–4:30, Sat. 1–11, 2–4:30, Sun. 2–4:30; closed Aug. and university holidays. Free.

William Holmes McGuffey (1800–73) was known to millions of Americans as the author of their reading primers and grade-school readers. The *First Eclectic Reader* appeared in 1836, and the series sold over a hundred million copies throughout the rest of the nineteenth century and well into the twentieth.

McGuffey was born in Washington County, Pennsylvania, but was brought by his parents to the Western Reserve (i.e., Ohio) in 1802. He was trained as a preacher and a teacher, and in 1826 was appointed a professor of languages at Miami University, which was then a one-building college in a pioneer village. He married Harriet Spining of Dayton in 1827, and the next year the couple purchased the lot on which they would build this house, needed for their growing family. The two-story brick house of six rooms, joined to an earlier frame house, was ready in 1833, and they moved in.

McGuffey spent ten years at Miami University. His first four readers were compiled in his home here; the selections were culled from his own writings, newspaper and magazine clippings, and excerpts from standard works, all intended not just to teach children how to read but to provide moral lessons at the same time. While he lived here he assembled neighborhood children and conducted classes with them as well as attending to his teaching assignments in Latin, Greek, and Hebrew at the university. He also made appearances on the lecture platform and in the pulpit. He was a member of the College of Professional Teachers of the Western Country, which held its annual meeting in Cincinnati. There he met other outstanding educators and writers, including Calvin Stowe (see Cincinnati). McGuffey resigned from the faculty of Miami University in 1836 to become president of Cincinnati College. He later became president of Ohio University in Athens, then returned to Cincinnati, and eventually became professor of moral philosophy at the University of Virginia, where he remained until his death.

The McGuffey Museum, a National Historic Landmark, is the house McGuffey built and resided in while at Miami. It has undergone a number of structural alterations since McGuffey lived here (the original frame house adjoining the brick portion was moved away, and mid-nineteenth-century owners replaced McGuffey's portico with a porch, changed the windows, and added Victorian decoration to the interior). No effort has been made to restore the house to the way it looked in McGuffey's time. Rather it has been refurbished to reflect the changes that would normally occur when a house has been lived in over a long period of time, so that while there are some furnishings circa 1833, there are also some from a later period. The furnishings in the downstairs library, however, all have McGuffey associations. The most outstanding piece is the octagonal desk McGuffey designed and had specially built. The top of the table turns so that any drawer can be easily reached. Many of the items in the room come from his home in Virginia. Portraits of McGuffey and his wife hang on the living room wall. The museum also has an extensive collection of McGuffey Readers and Spellers, some on display, and all available to researchers. The research collection also includes nineteenth-century textbooks, and manuscripts, letters, and diaries relating to McGuffey.

Ripley

Rankin House State Memorial. On Liberty Hill, overlooking the Ohio River. Apr.–Oct., Wed.–Sun. 9:30–5. Small admission.

The Reverend John Rankin, a Presbyterian minister, was one of the most ardent abolitionists in the days before the Civil War. His house on Liberty Hill, which was built in 1828, six years after he came to Ripley, was a station on the Underground Railroad, and from the time it was built until 1865 sheltered over two thousand escaped slaves on their way to freedom in the North and in Canada. Rankin had begun preaching against slavery as early as 1815, and his series of thirteen letters denouncing that "peculiar institution" appeared first in a local paper and then in book form as *Letters on American Slavery* (1826).

The Ordinance of 1787 had prohibited slavery in the Northwest Territory, of which Ohio was a part. This fact, together with Ripley's proximity to Kentucky, just across the Ohio River, made this place and other Ohio towns along the river (including Cincinnati) a logical first stop on the way to freedom. The Underground Railroad operation became risky for abolitionists with the passage of the Fugitive Slave Act of 1850, which made it illegal to harbor a runaway in free territory and enabled slave owners to cross into free territory to capture and bring back their property if ownership could be established. Nevertheless, Rankin and many others like him continued with their work, building secret passageways, using disguises, and otherwise outwitting slave catchers.

Rankin was friendly with the group of abolitionist ministers and educators centered in Cincinnati, and numbered among his close acquaintances the family of Lyman Beecher, father of Harriet Beecher Stowe (see Cincinnati). It was at this small red brick house that she was told the story of a slave woman who had carried her child over the frozen Ohio River and was saved when the ice thawed before her pursuers could catch up with her. This story was later incorporated into *Uncle Tom's Cabin* as the

"Eliza" episode. (The real Eliza was probably sheltered by the Quaker couple Levi and Catherine Coffin at their home in Fountain City, Indiana, another important stop on the Underground Railroad. The Coffin house is now an Indiana State Memorial; it is on US 27 and Mill St.; open June–Oct., Tues.–Sun. 1–4:30; admission.)

The Rankin house has been restored to commemorate the work of Rankin and Ohio's contribution to the struggle against slavery. It is a small, modest-looking house, simply furnished (some original pieces). The Rankin family Bible and other personal items are here, too. The exterior and interior are typical of a family dedicated more to spiritual ideals than to material possessions. The "stairway to liberty," a steep flight of wooden steps leading from the river bottomlands up to the house on the top of the hill—with a magnificent view of the Ohio River—has been rebuilt. Up these steps climbed the escaped slaves when they reached the Ohio shore and freedom.

OREGON

Oregon, like other northwestern states, makes its first appearance in American writing in the journals of Lewis and Clark (see Fort Clatsop, Astoria). The first truly literary work about Oregon is Washington Irving's *Astoria,* dealing with John Jacob Astor and his fur-trading settlement (see Astoria). Another noteworthy chronicle of exploration is John C. Frémont's *Report of the Exploring Expedition to the Rocky Mountains in the Year 1842, and to Oregon and Northern California in the Years 1843-44* (1845). Francis Parkman's classic, *The Oregon Trail* (1847), may be included in the literature of Oregon, but actually it is really about the eastern end of the great pioneer road and is more about Wyoming (see Fort Laramie, Wyoming) than anything else. Dr. John McLoughlin, called the "Father of Oregon," was the chief factor of the Hudson's Bay Company at Fort Vancouver (in Washington state) on the Columbia River, and ruled the Oregon Territory from 1824 to 1846. Eva Emery Dye wrote *McLoughlin and Old Oregon* and T. D. Allen is the author of *Troubled Border,* both historical novels about this man. His retirement home, built in 1846, is now the **McLoughlin House National Historic Site** in **Oregon City** (in McLoughlin Park, 713 Center Street at Seventh Street; Tues.–Sun. 10–4, 10–5 in summer; closed holidays; admission).

An interesting novel dealing with an Indian legend is *The Bridge of the Gods* (1890) by Frederic Homer Balch; it relates the Indian myth of the collapse of a stone bridge that supposedly spanned the Columbia River. Ernest Haycox of Portland was a prolific author of high-quality Westerns, several of which are laid in Oregon: *Canyon Passage, Long Storm,* and *The Earthbreak-*

ers. Perhaps the most outstanding novel of Oregon is *Honey in the Horn* by H. L. Davis, which won the Pulitzer Prize for fiction in 1936. It is a realistic historical novel about the homesteading period in Oregon in the early twentieth century.

The most colorful Oregon literary figure was Joaquin Miller, who arrived in Oregon with his family when he was thirteen. He first lived not far from present-day Eugene and spent much of his early life in Oregon (see Canyon City for more details). The influence of Miller's rather Byronic style can be seen in the work of Edwin Markham, who was born in Oregon City in 1852 (see San Jose, California).

John Reed, the journalist and poet whose best-known work is *Ten Days That Shook the World,* his eyewitness account of the Russian Revolution, came from an old and wealthy Oregon family; he was born and grew up in Portland. Three excellent and popular contemporary authors have Oregon backgrounds. Ken Kesey is a native Oregonian. His novels *One Flew Over the Cuckoo's Nest* and *Sometimes a Great Notion* were both filmed on location in the state. Ursula K. LeGuin, the distinguished science fiction writer, lives in Portland. Her novel *The Lathe of Heaven* is set in Portland in the year 2002. Richard Brautigan's *The Hawkline Monster: A Gothic Western* is set in eastern Oregon in 1902. William Stafford lives and teaches in Oregon, and much of the imagery of his poetry derives from the landscape of the Pacific Northwest.

Ashland

Oregon Shakespearean Festival. For ticket information write Oregon Shakespearean Festival Box Office, Ashland, OR 97520, or telephone 503-482-4331.

The Oregon Shakespearean Festival is one of the liveliest and best drama festivals in the country. Founded in 1935 by Angus L. Bowmer, it is the oldest event of its kind in the western hemisphere. There are three theaters. The Elizabethan Stage is an outdoor theater, a replica of the Fortune Theater of Shakespeare's London. Here the plays of Shakespeare are presented each summer. The Oregon Shakespearean Festival has performed the entire canon of Shakespeare's works twice since its founding, probably the only theater to accomplish this feat since Shakespeare's plays were first acted.

Two other theaters, both indoor, operate from February to April (the season called "Stage II") as well as in the summer: the Angus Bowmer and the Black Swan. At these two theaters other, non-Elizabethan plays as well as Shakespeare are performed, from Restoration comedy to contemporary drama. Recent productions have been of plays by Sheridan, Tennessee Williams, and Eugene O'Neill.

Backstage tours are available during Stage II (Saturdays) and the summer season (daily except Sundays); they begin at 10 a.m. and there is a charge. In the summer an Exhibit Center on the Southern Oregon State College campus is open, with displays about the more than forty years of festival history. A variety of talks, lectures, readings, dances, musical events, and other celebrations take place throughout the summer season; for details send for a brochure.

Astoria

Fort Clatsop National Memorial. 6 miles southwest of Astoria, just south of Business US 101. Daily; mid-June–Labor Day 8–8, rest of year 8–5; closed Christmas. Free.

On November 15, 1805, Meriwether Lewis and William Clark and their party sighted the Pacific Ocean, near what is now McGowan, Washington. They had reached their ultimate goal, after an arduous journey through the wilderness. On November 26 they crossed to the south shore of the Columbia River, where there was more game to kill for food. A scouting party canoed up a small tributary of the Columbia, now called the Lewis and Clark River, and established a campsite. Here the men began building

Fort Clatsop, which was ready by Christmas. They named their winter quarters for a friendly local Indian tribe, with whom they traded. The location afforded them an ample supply of meat, and they were able to obtain salt by boiling down seawater. It was not an ideal spot, however, the winter weather being constantly rainy.

During their sojourn at Fort Clatsop, Lewis and Clark brought their journals up to date and made copious notes on the flora and fauna they found in the vicinity. Clark drew maps of the enormous area they had traveled through—all the way from St. Louis. The party stayed at Fort Clatsop until spring. The meat supply was running low, the weather was getting warmer, and the men were anxious to begin their long journey back east. Fort Clatsop and its furnishings were presented to the Clatsop chief as a token of friendship and thanks, and on March 23, 1806, the expedition started back up the Columbia River in their canoes.

Fort Clatsop National Memorial is a replica of the original fort, no traces of which have survived. The replica was built in 1955 on the sesquicentennial of the Lewis and Clark expedition, and follows the floor plan drawn by Clark on the elk-hide cover of his field book. There is an exhibit room with a narrated slide program that explains the expedition. Besides the fort, a replica of a thirty-two-foot dugout canoe used by Lewis and Clark is displayed at the canoe landing. Demonstrations of flintlock rifle loading and firing, preparation of food, carving, and other activities are given by costumed interpreters during the summer season. (Picnic area available.)

Fort Astoria. Exchange and Fourteenth Streets. Daily in summer, Tues.–Sun. in winter, 10:30–5. Small admission.

In 1811 agents of John Jacob Astor came to the mouth of the Columbia River and established a fur-trading post only a few miles from the site of Fort Clatsop, at what is now the city of Astoria. The venture was short-lived, since the War of 1812 forced Astor to dissolve the associations he had with British traders and the fort passed into the hands of the British (American control was restored in 1818). Many years later, in 1834, when Astor was the richest man in America, he had the idea of having a book written about his venture, and engaged Washington Irving, the most famous writer in America, to do the job. Irving was criticized at the time for being a paid glorifier of Astor, and it is true that in *Astoria,* published in 1836, he shows Astor in nothing but the best light. Astor supplied him with research materials and paid the author handsomely. Irving's nephew, Pierre Munro Irving, aided in the research, and it is also a fact that much of *Astoria,* particularly the historical background sections, consists of narratives from other sources. A third criticism is that the book does not strictly adhere to fact, and that when solid information was lacking, Irving made do with imagination and invention, even though the book purports to be authoritative reportage. Nevertheless, in spite of these drawbacks, *Astoria, or, Anecdotes of an Enterprise Beyond the Rocky Mountains* was extremely successful in its day, went through several editions, and was translated into a number of languages. It can still be read with pleasure.

Fort Astoria is the partially restored outpost established by John Jacob Astor's fur-trading company, with a museum.

The **Astoria Column** (follow signs on scenic drive to Coxcomb Hill) is a 125-foot tower dedicated to early settlements in Astoria. A frieze around the column depicts Lewis and Clark, Astor's fur-trading post, and other historic scenes. The observation tower (free) is open daily 8–8, in summer to 10 p.m.; information booth open daily in summer, 9–6.

Canyon City

Joaquin Miller Cabin. At Herman and Eliza Oliver Historical Museum, on US 395, 2 miles south of John Day. Apr.–May, Sept.–Oct., Tues.–Sat. 9–3; June–Aug., daily 9–3. Small admission.

Cincinnatus Hiner (or Heine) Miller, later known as Joaquin Miller, was born in 1839 in Indiana. In 1852 his family traveled westward and settled in Oregon near present-day Eugene. Young Miller—"Nat," as he was then called—ran away from home when he was seventeen to begin a life of adventure. He worked in the California mining camps, went to live with an Indian tribe in the vicinity of Mount Shasta in northern California, "married" an Indian woman, who bore him a daughter. After a number of Indian disturbances in the region it became unsafe for a white sympathizer to remain, and Miller returned to Oregon. He attended an academy called Columbia College in Portland for a while, then became a schoolteacher in Clarke, Washington Territory. He studied law and was admitted to the bar in Portland in 1861. In 1862 he established a pony express between Washington and Idaho and made enough money to enable him to purchase the *Democratic Register* in Eugene in 1863. In his first editorial he defended Joaquin Murietta, the Mexican bandit, and earned himself the nickname Joaquin, which he eventually came to use as his pen name. He also published some of his verse, which was admired by another poet, Minnie Theresa Dyer of Port Orford, who had also published in the Eugene papers. A series of letters of mutual admiration between the two resulted in Miller's going down to meet the girl, and within a week he married Minnie Myrtle, as he called her.

Miller supported the Confederacy in his editorials, and for this reason the newspaper was suppressed during the Civil War. In 1863 he went east to Canyon City, a mining town where gold had been discovered in 1862. He led the townspeople against a band of Indians who had been stealing cattle and horses and harassing the town, and was elected judge of the Grant County court in 1866, serving until 1869. His wife bore two children during this period, but the couple separated, and she divorced him in 1869. While at Canyon City he published his first two volumes of poetry, *Specimens* (1868) and *Joaquin et al* (1869). He went to San Francisco in 1870 and joined the literary circle of Bret Harte, and then went on to a career as the "poet of the Sierras" and a very colorful personality. Aside from his volumes of poetry he published a prose autobiography, *Life Amongst the Modocs,* in 1873, which contains material about his life in Oregon, although with his tendency toward exaggeration, it is not too reliable.

The Oliver Historical Museum has exhibits about the miners and settlers of the 1860s. Adjacent to the museum is the 1865 cabin where Joaquin Miller lived when he came to Canyon City. (For more about Miller see Oakland, California.)

SOUTH DAKOTA

The pioneer settlers have, quite naturally, been the main subject matter of South Dakota literature. One of the outstanding works is Ole Rölvaag's *Giants in the Earth* (first published in Norwegian in 1924–25 and in English in 1927), a novel of stark realism about Norwegian immigrant farmers who trek from Minnesota to the Dakota Territory and undergo many hardships. It is the first book of a trilogy that continues with *Peder Victorious* and *Their Father's God.*

Hamlin Garland also gave realistic accounts of the struggles of the pioneers in South Dakota in his many books about the Middle West. Garland, born in Wisconsin (see West Salem, Wisconsin), moved to South Dakota with his family when he was a young man. He lived intermittently at his family's homestead near Ordway, a tiny town not far from Aberdeen, from 1881 to 1884. In 1883 he filed a claim of his own for a homestead a few miles from his father's. During this period he first began writing. His poems, stories, novels, and autobiographical writings are filled with the scenes and characters he knew here. *Main-Travelled Roads* (1891) contains stories and sketches of the grim struggles of the farmers of the Dakotas and Iowa, and realistically depicts the drudgery and ugliness of homestead life. It was at first attacked in the Midwest, but was highly praised in the East, particularly by William Dean Howells. *The Moccasin Ranch* is a novel by Garland about homesteading in "Boomtown" (Ordway). His later autobiographical writings, *A Son of the Middle Border, A Daughter of the Middle Border,* and other "Middle Border" books also graphically depict the hard life of the pioneer on the prairie. After Garland proved his homestead claim he mortgaged it for two hundred dollars and used the money to travel east. The site of the Garland family homestead is identified by a marker two miles north and a half mile west of the old town of Ordway in Brown County, northeast of Aberdeen.

Another resident of Aberdeen was L. Frank Baum, later author of *The Wizard of Oz.* As a young man he operated a variety and candy store and also edited the *Saturday Pioneer,* a weekly newspaper in which he wrote humorous columns. Eventually, though, the paper went broke, and Baum moved on.

Laura Ingalls Wilder wrote about the pioneers in her famous "Little House" books for children. She came from De Smet (which see), where her daughter, Rose Wilder Lane, also a writer, was born.

Another homesteader was Oscar Micheaux, a black author and film maker. He homesteaded on the Rosebud Reservation at the beginning of the century. He wrote *The Conquest* and *The Homesteader,* among others.

Western South Dakota, in the Black Hills, was the Wild West in the nineteenth century and was the scene of a gold rush in 1876. The town of **Deadwood** (now a tourist attraction) is known for Calamity Jane and Wild Bill Hickok, subjects of many Westerns. In August 1876 Jack McCall fatally shot Hickok in the back in a Deadwood saloon. Hickok, Calamity Jane, Preacher Smith, and other characters are buried in Mt. Moriah Cemetery, the Boot Hill of Deadwood. *The Trial of Jack McCall* is acted throughout the summer at the Old Town Hall. Stewart Edward White (1873–1946) wrote several novels about the gold-mining days. The mining town of Keystone, in the Black Hills northeast of Custer, provided the setting for his novel *The Claim Jumpers; Gold* and *The Westerners* were also about prospectors. *The Legend of Devil's Gulch,* a play about the gold rush, is performed at the Black Hills Playhouse in the summer (see Custer State Park).

The "Western" aspect of South Dakota writing is epitomized in the work of Badger Clark, the late poet laureate of South Dakota (see Custer State Park again).

The story of the Indians of the Dakotas has been the subject of many fine books. Mari Sandoz (see Gordon, Nebraska) wrote *Crazy Horse,* about the Sioux chief who led his people against Custer (see Montana). John G. Neihardt's *Black Elk Speaks* is a collection of lore about the Oglala Sioux (see Bancroft, Nebraska). Stanley Vestal wrote *Sitting Bull: Champion of the Sioux,* about the great chief. On the Oglala Sioux reservation (headquarters at Pine Ridge) is **Wounded Knee Battlefield** (8 miles east on US 18, then 7 miles north on an unnumbered road), where on December 29, 1890, hundreds of Sioux, including women and children, were massacred by soldiers of the 7th Cavalry. This atrocity marked the end of armed confrontation between the U.S. government and the Sioux nation. A monument to the slain marks their mass grave. Dee Brown's *Bury My Heart at Wounded Knee: An Indian History of the American West* takes its title from this tragic event. Vine Deloria, an Oglala Sioux born in Martin, South Dakota, is another Native American author who has written of the history of the Indian-white conflict from the Indian point of view; *Custer Died for Your Sins* is one of his best-known works.

Among contemporary writers, Frederick Manfred (who first wrote under the pen name of Feike Feikema) has been most successful in transforming the matter of South Dakota history into fiction. He has written of the Sioux in *Conquering Horse* and *Scarlet Plume* and of the Black Hills gold rush in *King of Spades.* *Lord Grizzly* is a fictional treatment of the story of Hugh Glass, a hunter and guide with an expedition led by General William A. Ashley. In the summer of 1823 Glass was scouting ahead near the forks of the Grand River when he was attacked by a grizzly bear. A terrible fight took place; when Glass's companions found him, he was unconscious and seriously injured; the bear was dead. Two men were left behind to care for him, but when Glass failed to regain consciousness, they abandoned him, taking his weapons with them. But Glass did come to, realized he had been abandoned, and swore to get revenge on those who had deserted him. He discovered he had a broken leg, and realized that to save himself he would have to crawl to the nearest settlement, at Fort Kiowa on the Missouri River. He arrived there after weeks of incredible suffering and endurance. After recovering from his ordeal he set out to find the men who had left him for dead, but when he finally caught up with them, he forgave them. This epic story of courage was also the subject of *The Song of Hugh Glass* by John G. Neihardt (see Bancroft, Nebraska).

Custer State Park

3 miles east of Custer on US 16A. Park season runs Memorial Day–Labor Day, but buildings may be open before and after these dates. Entrance fee. Camping at 9 locations within park.

This 72,000-acre park (which is just south of Mt. Rushmore) is one of the largest state parks in the country. In addition to its profusion of wildlife and the usual outdoor activities, the park has historical and cultural interest. The Gordon Stockade is a replica of the original fort built by the first white settlers in the Black Hills, who had entered illegally in search of gold in 1874. After a hard winter, the cavalry arrested them and escorted them out of these hills.

At the famous **Black Hills Playhouse,** *The Legend of Devil's Gulch* by Dr. Warren M. Lee, a "historical fantasy" about the real events that led to the settling of the Black Hills during the gold rush of 1875–76, is presented on several evenings during the summer. On other nights contemporary plays and musicals are performed June through August. (Information available at Visitor Center of Park, or write to Black Hills Playhouse, Custer, SD 57730 in summer, or College of Fine Arts, University of South Dakota, Vermillion, SD 57069 rest of year.)

The Badger Hole was the home for thirty years of Badger Clark (1883–1957), the poet laureate of South Dakota. In *Sun and Saddle Leather, Sky Lines and Wood Smoke, Spike,* and other collections of poems he wrote of the West and especially of the beauty of the Black Hills. His most famous poems are probably "The Cowboy's Prayer," "The Job," and "The Glory Trail." He lived alone in this cabin, which he built with his own hands, for about thirty years. The contents of the Badger Hole, which is near the intersection of US 16 and SR 87 in the park, remain exactly as they were when he lived here.

De Smet

Laura Ingalls Wilder Memorial. May 1–Oct. 15. Admission includes tour map and guided tour of Surveyor's House and Ingalls Home.

De Smet (named after Father P. J. De Smet, a missionary who traveled throughout the West in the early nineteenth century and wrote several volumes about his experiences) is in eastern South Dakota. It is the *Little Town on the Prairie* of Laura Ingalls Wilder. In the "Little House" series of beloved children's books Wilder told the story of her pioneer family and their early struggles. Six volumes of the series take place in and around De Smet. The Laura Ingalls Wilder Memorial Society has a tour of the town covering the various sites that appear in the books. The tour begins at the restored Surveyor's House (at Olivet and First Sts.), the little frame structure where the Ingalls family spent their first fall and winter here (described in *By the Shores of Silver Lake*). It continues to the City Library, where Ingalls mementos and five paintings by the South Dakota artist Harvey Dunn, also from De Smet, are on display. The tour passes the sites of stores mentioned in the books and then goes on to the Ingalls home, where the family lived from 1887 to 1928. This too has been restored and has exhibits about the author.

Just east of town (take Highway 14) is the site of the Ingalls homestead, where the family lived in a "claim shanty" in 1880 before they moved back to town to spend *The Long Winter;* a memorial plaque has been placed on a rock here. Nearby is the site of the Laura Ingalls Wilder Pageant, *The Long Winter,* presented in late June and early July (no advance tickets sold; inquire at the Surveyor's House headquarters).

About a mile and a half north of town is the Wilder homestead site, where Laura Ingalls moved after she married Almanzo Wilder (the subject of *These Happy Golden Years*). Her daughter Rose Wilder Lane was born in their claim shanty there. (Rose

Wilder Lane's *Let the Hurricane Roar* and *Free Land* tell the story of South Dakota pioneers in the 1870s and 1880s.) Two other books in the Laura Ingalls Wilder series also tell of life in De Smet: *The First Four Years* and *On the Way Home*. In 1894 Laura and Almanzo, with their daughter, left De Smet to settle in Mansfield, Missouri (which see).

North of town is the De Smet Cemetery, where many Ingalls family members are buried (Laura and Almanzo are buried in Mansfield), as well as other persons identified in the Wilder books.

Mitchell

Museum of Pioneer Life. 1311 South Duff, on campus of Dakota Wesleyan University. June–Sept., Mon.–Sat. 8 a.m.–9 p.m., Sun. 1–9; lecture nightly in summer; open by appointment rest of year. Admission.

The Museum of Pioneer Life in Mitchell (the town where the famous Corn Palace is located) was founded by Hamlin Garland, John Dewey, and the historian James Truslow Adams, among others. It has manuscripts of O. E. Rölvaag, John G. Neihardt, Rose Wilder Lane, L. Frank Baum, Hamlin Garland, and Frederick Manfred, as well as paintings by the Sioux artist Oscar Howe, Harvey Dunn of South Dakota, and other Western artists. Major exhibits depict Indian and pioneer life in the Dakota Territory. (The museum was originally called the Friends of the Middle Border Museum, after Hamlin Garland's books.)

UTAH

Three great subjects dominate the literature about Utah: the vast, monumental deserts, rivers, and canyons of Utah in its natural state; the Old West of rough-and-tumble days; and of course, the saga of the Mormon migration and settlement.

Those interested in the early explorers of this once forbidding territory should read John Wesley Powell's *Exploration of the Colorado River of the West and Its Tributaries* (1875). Powell made a trip on the Colorado and Green Rivers in 1869, and this book, although originally a government report, by no means reads like one, but rather is a great document in the literature of exploration. He published another volume, *Canyons of the Colorado,* in 1895. The Green River empties into the Colorado River in Canyonlands National Park; the Colorado then flows through Glen Canyon National Recreation Area and becomes Lake Powell (named after the explorer) before narrowing at the Arizona border, where it flows through the Grand Canyon.

One of the most important events in the winning of the West took place in Utah when a golden spike was driven through the rails on May 10, 1869, near Promontory, Utah, to complete the first transcontinental railroad. **Golden Spike National Historic Site** (about 30 miles west of Brigham City on SR 83, then west on unnumbered road to Promontory) has a Visitor Center with a film and exhibits (June–Aug., daily 8–8; Apr.–May, Sept.–Oct., Mon.–Fri. 8–4:30, Sat. and Sun. 8–6; Nov.–Mar., daily 8–4:30). Several times a day in summer the original ceremony is reenacted. Of the many Westerns in which this event figures, the best-known are two about the building of the Union Pacific Railroad: Zane Grey's *The U.P. Trail* and Ernest Haycox's *Trouble Shooter.*

Zane Grey visited **Kanab,** Utah, in 1908, and lived there while he was writing his most famous book, *Riders of the Purple Sage.* The town is at the foot of the Vermillion Cliffs, and with its canyons and sand dunes is so picturesque that scores of movies have been filmed here. Inquire locally for the nearby locations of the several movie sets, with false-front streets and an old fort. Guided tours are also available locally. (Monument Valley, south of the San Juan River toward the Arizona border, is the setting for all those John Ford movies.)

Some other Westerns with a Utah setting are *Utah Blaine* by Jim Mayo (a pseudonym of the prolific Louis L'Amour), *Fort Starvation* by Frank Gruber, and *Rimrock* by Luke Short, the last about uranium prospecting. Wallace Stegner, one of America's most distinguished writers on Western subjects, is the author of *The Big Rock Candy Mountain* (1943), set in part in Utah. The real Big Rock Candy Mountain, rounded and chocolate- and lemon-colored, is seven miles south of Sevier on US 89.

The historian Bernard DeVoto was born in Ogden in 1897. His great trilogy about the westward expansion comprises *The Year of Decision: 1846, Across the Wide Missouri* (Pulitzer Prize, 1948), and *The Course of Empire.* He also wrote several novels set in the West: *The Crooked Mile, The House of the Sun-Goes-Down,* and *Mountain Time.*

Many historical novels have been written about the Mormon migration to "Deseret," one of the most distinguished of which is Vardis Fisher's *Children of God* (1939), which won the Harper Prize. This epic novel begins with the youth of Joseph Smith and follows the story with the leadership of Brigham Young and through to the late nineteenth century. (Curiously, Arthur Conan Doyle's first Sherlock Holmes story, *A Study in Scarlet,* published in 1887, has a tale about Mormons—shown in a cruelly uncomplimentary light—as the key to the mystery.) Among recent histories about the Mormons is Wallace Stegner's *Gathering of Zion: The Story of the Mormon Trail* (1964). Monuments and historic relics of the Mormons can be found throughout Utah, but a visitor's interest is naturally centered in Salt Lake City.

Salt Lake City

Brigham Young and his followers arrived at the site that was to become their home in 1847. **"This is the Place" Monument** at the mouth of Emigration Canyon (east on Sunnyside Avenue in Pioneer State Park) is a huge granite and bronze memorial erected in 1947 on the centennial of the city's founding. One of the oldest homes in Salt Lake City is the **Old Log House,** built in 1847, and preserved (but not open to the public) on the southeast corner of Temple Square.

The early Mormons were persecuted and hated by many, and were a curiosity to all "gentiles" (non-Mormons), particularly because of their practice of polygamy. Among early visitors to Salt Lake City was the ubiquitous Mark Twain, then still Sam Clemens, on his way to Nevada in 1862. Although he was, to say the least, skeptical about their religious beliefs, he admired the Mormons for their industry and the attractiveness of their city. He describes it in *Roughing It:*

> Next day we strolled about everywhere through the broad, straight, level streets, and enjoyed the pleasant strangeness of a city of fifteen thousand inhabitants with no loafers perceptible in it; and no visible drunkards or noisy people; a limpid stream rippling and dancing through every street in place of a filthy gutter; block after block of trim dwellings, built of "frame" and sunburned brick—a great thriving orchard and garden behind every one of them—apparently branches from the street stream winding and sparkling among the garden beds and fruit trees—and a grand general air of neatness, repair, thrift and comfort, around and about and over the whole. And everywhere were workshops, factories, and all manner of industries; and intent faces and busy hands were to be seen wherever one looked; and in one's ears was the ceaseless clink of hammers, the buzz of trade and the contented hum of drums and fly-wheels.

He saw the **Beehive House,** which had been built as a residence for Brigham Young, his wives and children (at South Temple and

State Streets; open to the public daily; free) and the **Lion House** next door, another residence for Brigham's family.

A year later, in 1863, another great humorist, Charles Farrar Browne, better known as Artemus Ward, showed up in Salt Lake City during one of his famous lecture tours. He fell ill in Utah and was nursed by a Mormon woman, and during his recovery he had time to observe the life of the Mormons, who became one of the chief topics of his enormously popular lectures. His lecture on the Mormons, in which he ridiculed them in his typically deadpan manner, later appeared in book form as *Artemus Ward among the Mormons.*

Sir Richard Burton, the great English explorer and travel writer, made a trip to the American West in 1860 and spent some three weeks in Salt Lake City. His observations and judgments of the Mormons can be found in *The City of the Saints and Across the Rocky Mountains to California,* published in England in 1861.

Another English visitor to Salt Lake City was Oscar Wilde, who came here during his American lecture tour in 1882. In a letter he wrote:

> I have lectured to the Mormons—the Opera House at Salt Lake City is an enormous affair about the size of Covent Garden, and holds with ease 14 families. . . . The President, a nice old man, sat with 5 wives in the stage box. I visited him in the afternoon and saw a charming daughter of his.

Wilde also saw the **Tabernacle,** built in 1867. He remarked that

> it is in the shape of a soup-kettle. It is decorated by the only native artist, and he has treated religious subjects in the naive spirit of the early Florentine painters, representing people of our own day in the dress of the period side by side with people of Biblical history who are clothed in some romantic costume.

Maps for walking and driving tours of Salt Lake City can be obtained at the **Visitor Center** on Temple Square; or write Salt Lake Valley Convention & Visitors Bureau, The Salt Palace, Suite 200, Salt Lake City, UT 84101, or Utah Travel Council, Council Hall, Salt Lake City, UT 84114.

WASHINGTON

After the Lewis and Clark expeditions, the history of Washington is dominated for decades by the fur traders. **Fort Vancouver** (now a National Historic Site in Vancouver, on East Evergreen Boulevard; Mon–Fri. 8–5, Sat., Sun., and holidays 9–5; closed Thanksgiving, Christmas, and New Year's Day; free) was established by the Hudson's Bay Company. Not just a fort but the center of a community of tradesmen and workers as well as soldiers, with schools, churches, and dwellings surrounding the actual fort, it was ruled over for over twenty years by Dr. John McLoughlin, chief factor of the Hudson's Bay Company (see Oregon), the subject of *McLoughlin and Old Oregon* by Eva Emery Dye and *Troubled Border* by T. D. Allen. John C. Frémont stopped at Fort Vancouver when he traveled down the Columbia River during his 1843 expedition to the Oregon Territory and northern California.

Two regional writers who have specialized in books with Washington State settings are Nard Jones and Archie Binns. Jones wrote *Evergreen Land,* a nonfiction work about the state. His novel *The Petlands* used Seattle as a setting, and *Wheat Women* takes place in the area around Walla Walla; *Swift Flows the River* is about steamboating on the Columbia River, and *Scarlet Petticoat* is about the early fur-trading days. Binns, in addition to nonfiction works like *The Sea and the Forest,* about Puget Sound, wrote the novel *Lightship,* laid in the Puget Sound area, and *The Laurels Are Cut Down,* which takes place on the Olympic peninsula (good reading for a trip to **Olympic National Park**). *Mighty Mountain* is set in Olympia and around Mount Rainier in the 1850s (reading for **Mount Rainier National Park**). Bill Gulick is another Washington writer, whose novel *Bend of the Snake* takes place in the area of that river in southeast Washington.

Former Supreme Court Justice William O. Douglas grew up in Yakima, and has written of the great outdoors of Washington in *Of Men and Mountains,* about his experiences in the Cascades, and in *My Wilderness: The Pacific Northwest.*

Seattle has an interesting history. **Pioneer Square** (First Avenue at James Street) is the heart of old Seattle. It was the site of a sawmill, and the term "skid row," originally "skid road," referred to the hill down which logs were slid to the waterfront. Seattle was the starting point for the 1898 Alaska gold rush, and is now the starting point for the Klondike Gold Rush National Park, with a Visitor Center at 117 South Main Street, in the Pioneer Square Historic District (see Alaska). For tourist information about Seattle contact Seattle & Kings County Convention & Visitors Bureau (1815 Seventh Avenue, Seattle, WA 98101). Edna Ferber's *Great Son* (1945) is a historical novel about a Seattle family through several generations.

Although his poetry is not at all regional, Theodore Roethke is associated with Washington. The Pulitzer Prize-winning poet taught at the University of Washington at Seattle, where he lived until his death in 1963. David Wagoner is another distinguished Washington poet whose work reflects his Pacific Northwest background. The recently published *Who Shall Be the Sun?* is subtitled *Poems Based on the Lore, Legends, and Myths of Northwest Coast and Plateau Indians.*

A recent, charming book is *Oysterville* by Willard R. Espy, an account of how the author's forebears came to the tiny village of Oysterville on a peninsula between Willapa Bay and the Pacific Ocean. And a very popular contemporary novelist, Tom Robbins, makes his home in Washington; *Another Roadside Attraction* takes place (so to speak) in the state.

Walla Walla

Whitman Mission National Historic Site. 7 miles west of Walla Walla, then short drive via connecting road south from US 12. Daily, Memorial Day–Labor Day, 8–8, rest of year, 8–4:30; closed Thanksgiving, Christmas, New Year's Day. Free.

The story of the Whitman Mission is one of the most dramatic in the history of the Pacific Northwest. It was founded at Waiilatpu ("the place of the people of the rye grass") among the Cayuse Indians in 1836 by Marcus and Narcissa Whitman, Protestant missionaries sent by the American Board of Commissioners for Foreign Missions. At that period the Oregon territory, of which this area was a part, was known among whites only by explorers and fur traders. In 1935 Marcus Whitman and Reverend Samuel Parker had come out to Oregon country to select sites for missions among the Indians. Whitman returned east while Parker continued to explore, and in 1836, Whitman returned with his new wife Narcissa, Reverend Henry Spalding and his wife Eliza, and William Gray. Eliza and Narcissa were the first white women to cross the continent overland.

Spalding established his mission among the Nez Perce at Lapwai, near present-day Lewiston, Idaho, while Whitman set up his here on this site. Aside from religious conversion, the missionaries saw as one of their goals the education of the Indians; they devised alphabets for the Nez Perce and Spokan languages, and printed books in these languages at a press at Lapwai, beginning in 1839; these were the first books to be printed in the Pacific Northwest.

The mission grew. An adobe house, a sawmill, a gristmill, and a blacksmith shop were built and put into operation. The Indians, however, were largely indifferent to the Whitmans' efforts at conversion and teaching, preferring to adhere to their nomadic way of life and old traditions. In 1842 the American Board decided to close the Waiilatpu and Lapwai missions, but Whitman, determined to keep them open, made a six-month journey to Boston, where he succeeded in convincing his superiors that the stations should continue in operation. On his way back, Whitman joined a wagon train in the Great Migration to Oregon, which by 1843 had made the Oregon Trail the most important westward road for the pioneers. The Whitman mission served as a way station on the route of the emigrants, and even after 1844, when the main route bypassed the mission, the sick and those in trouble found refuge there.

All this good work came to an end on November 29, 1847. The Cayuse were in a state of unrest. They feared that the white settlers were planning to take their land (a not entirely unfounded suspicion). A measles epidemic had decimated the tribe, and they suspected, wrongly, of course, that the medicine Dr. Whitman gave them was really poison. On that day in November, a group of Cayuse attacked the mission, killed Marcus and Narcissa Whitman and eleven others, and destroyed the mission buildings. The result of the massacre was an end of Protestant missionary work among the Indians of the Oregon country and a war against the Cayuse. A more positive result was the vote in Congress to create the Territory of Oregon in August 1848, an act that gave the territory a formal government.

The Whitman Mission National Historic Site has a Visitor Center with a museum and the common grave of the Whitmans and the others who were killed. Self-guiding foot trails lead to the actual mission site, and a Memorial Shaft is dedicated to those who died.

Books about the Whitmans are Nard Jones's nonfiction *Marcus Whitman: The Great Command;* historical novels by T. D. Allen (*Doctor in Buckskin*), Honoré Willsie Morrow (*We Must March*), and Paul Cranston (*To Heaven on Horseback*); also *Narcissa Whitman* by Opal Sweazea Allen.

WISCONSIN

The story of the pioneer settlers of Wisconsin has been told by Hamlin Garland in *A Son of the Middle Border* and other writings (see West Salem). The "Little House" books for children by Laura Ingalls Wilder begin in Wisconsin; the first volume in the series is *Little House in the Big Woods,* which tells the story of her childhood in Wisconsin. An official marker in a park at Pepin commemorates her contribution to children's literature (see also De Smet, South Dakota, and Mansfield, Missouri). Another famous children's book is *Caddie Woodlawn* by Carol Ryrie Brink, also set in pioneer Wisconsin (see Downsville).

Two prominent women novelists had Wisconsin origins. Zona Gale was born and lived in Portage (which see). Edna Ferber was born in Kalamazoo, grew up in Appleton, and worked as a young reporter in Milwaukee. Ferber's first novel *Dawn O'Hara* is based in part on this period in her life. *Fanny, Herself* is a quasi-autobiographical novel about a Jewish girl growing up in Winnebago at the turn of the century. *A Peculiar Treasure* (1938), her autobiography, tells of her girlhood in Wisconsin.

Another Wisconsin writer is Glenway Wescott, who although he lived abroad for many years, used his home state as the locale for several books. The main character of *The Apple of the Eye* (1924) is a Wisconsin farm boy; *The Grandmothers* (1927) portrays a pioneer Wisconsin family; and *Goodbye, Wisconsin* (1928) is a collection of short stories.

The writer who has used Wisconsin material the most widely and deeply is August Derleth (1909–71), best known for his "Sac Prairie Saga," a long series of volumes of fiction and poetry tracing the life of a Wisconsin community from its settlement in 1830 to the present. He modeled Sac Prairie on his hometown, **Sauk City,** where a plaque has been dedicated to him. *Wind Over Wisconsin* is chronologically the first volume in this important series of regional writings; *Still Is the Summer Night* and *Restless Is the River* are two other novels in the Sac Prairie saga; *Sac Prairie People* is a collection of short stories. Derleth has written other books with a Wisconsin background, including *Bright Journey* and its sequel, *The House on the Mound,* historical novels mainly about Hercules Dousman, an early Wisconsin fur trader and the region's first millionaire. The fabulously lavish **Villa Louis** in Prairie du Chien (off US 18 at 521 North Villa Louis Road; open May–Oct., daily 9–5; admission) was built in 1843 by Dousman as a gift for his bride, Jane Fisher Dousman, who became famous for parties that equaled the lavishness of the house. Now a museum, it contains beautiful Waterford crystal chandeliers, elegant hand-carved rosewood furniture, a large library, and an art collection. (The house was built on an enormous Hopewell Indian burial mound, and the carriage house now contains a museum about the Hopewell culture, with additional exhibits on the early fur trade.) These last two books by Derleth, as well as *The Hills Stand Watch,* among others, are part of the author's "Wisconsin Saga."

For those interested in the Native American culture of Wisconsin, *The Autobiography of a Winnebago Indian* (1920) by the great anthropologist Paul Radin is recommended.

Downsville

Caddie Woodlawn Memorial Park. On SR 25, 12 miles south of Menomonie. Open daily. Free.

Caddie Woodlawn by Carol Ryrie Brink, which won the Newbery Award as the most distinguished children's book of the year in 1935, has been a favorite with young readers for years. The original for Caddie Woodlawn was Mrs. Brink's grandmother Carolina Augusta Woodhouse, who at the age of four, in 1857, came with her family to the wilds of Wisconsin. The family settled on a homestead here near the Menomonie (now Red Cedar) River. *Caddie Woodlawn* and its sequel, *Magical Melons,* tell the story of the pioneer girl and her family on the 160-acre farm. The house where the Woodhouse family lived (moved in 1970 from its original site about 300 yards to the east) is preserved by the Dunn County Historical Society in a park on a portion of the original acreage. Within the park Mary Woodhouse, Caroline's sister, who died at the age of seven shortly after her arrival here, is buried.

East of the park are the remnants of the tiny village of Dunnville, where steamers once loaded and unloaded on the river, and where Caddie went to school. A booklet entitled *Caddie Woodlawn: A Pioneer Girl on Wisconsin's Frontier,* available from the Dunn County Historical Society (Box 437, Menomonie, WI 54751) gives a brief description of this pioneer western Wisconsin community and has a map of Caddie Woodlawn country.

Portage

Zona Gale (1874–1938) was born in Portage. She started her career as a reporter first in Milwaukee and later for the New York *World,* but eventually devoted her full time to creative writing. She is known especially for her realistic works dealing with small-town middle western life. The Friendship Village of her fiction is based on her hometown. In her best-known work, the short novel *Miss Lulu Bett* (the dramatization of which won her the Pulitzer Prize for drama in 1921), she portrayed a woman exploited by her family as a household drudge until she rebels; it could be called an early feminist novel. Gale outgrew the sentimentality of her early work to become an important voice in the generation of Sinclair Lewis, during the 1920s, exposing the hypocrisies and crassness of the small-town bourgeoisie. Other books by her are *Bridal Pond, Birth, Neighbors, Neighborhood Stories, Friendship Village Love Stories,* and the nonfiction *Portage, Wisconsin, and Other Essays. Still Small Voice* is a biography of Zona Gale by the Wisconsin author August Derleth.

Three houses in Portage have Zona Gale associations. Her birthplace is at **605 DeWitt Street,** and has a plaque placed by the Portage Lively Arts Council. When Zona Gale returned to Portage to live there in 1912 she resided at **506 West Edgewater,** a house overlooking the Wisconsin River. At one time she also lived in the building now occupied by the **Portage Free Public Library** at the corner of West Franklin and MacFarlane Road.

Portage also has a number of other sites of literary interest. The name of the town derives from the fact that it lies at the point where the Indians and then the early French explorers Marquette and Jolliet and early trappers had to portage their canoes between the Fox and Wisconsin rivers (a canal was built in 1876 but is now closed). The **Old Indian Agency House** (1 mile east of Portage off SR 33; May–Oct., daily 9–5, winter by appointment; small admission) was the house built in 1832 for John Kinzie, agent to the Winnebago Indians, and his wife Juliette. Restored and operated by the Wisconsin Society of Colonial Dames, it is a fine example of early-nineteenth-century architecture. Furnishings include antique period pieces, piano, Hitchcock chairs, and household articles, plus a collection of Indian artifacts. Juliette Kinzie was the author of *Wau-Bun,* an excellent narrative record of life in early Wisconsin, and an important historical document. Nearby (on SR 33) is the site of old **Fort Winnebago,** erected in 1828. The only remaining building is the Surgeon's Quarters (open May–Oct., daily 9–5, winter by appointment; small admission).

Portage was also the home of two other distinguished writers. Frederick Jackson Turner (1861–1932), the historian famous for his frontier hypothesis of American history, lived at one time at **319 West Franklin** (not open to visitors). Portage Turner High School is named for him. John Muir (see Martinez, California), the great naturalist, lived on a farm now marked by the **County Park** outside Portage. **Muir View,** on South Highway 51 in Poynette, marked by a monument, is a panoramic view of the Wisconsin River and its bluffs.

West Salem

Hamlin Garland Homestead. 357 West Garland Street. Memorial Day–Sept. 15, Mon.–Sat. 10–7; other times by appointment (telephone 608-786-1399). Admission.

Hamlin Garland was born in 1860 in West Salem, La Crosse County, in a log cabin. In the spring of 1861 his pioneer family moved to Green's Coulee, a few miles west of here near Onalaska, and settled on a farm, where they lived until 1869. In that year Hamlin's father, dissatisfied with the small productivity of the farm, moved his family to Iowa, where Garland graduated from Cedar Valley Seminary in Osage in 1881. In that same year his family moved yet again, this time to a homestead in the Dakotas (see Aberdeen, South Dakota). By this time Garland was grown up and had taken to the road and a variety of jobs as teacher, salesman, carpenter, and homesteader in Dakota Territory. Eventually he went to Boston to further his education, enrolling at the Boston School of Oratory. During his sojourn in Boston, from 1884 to 1889, he taught and lectured and became acquainted with many prominent Boston literary figures, including William Dean Howells and Oliver Wendell Holmes. An 1887 return visit to the Midwest planted the seeds in his mind for his future writings, for on this trip he observed the life of the farmers of Wisconsin, Iowa, and the Dakotas with a fresh eye. In the life of his parents and other settlers of the region he saw hardship and drudgery unrelieved by art, beauty, or joy. On this trip he began writing the stories that would present a vividly realistic portrait of the life of unremitting struggle on the farms of the "middle border," which, he would later explain, "does not exist and never did. It was but a vaguely defined region even in my boyhood. It was the line drawn by the plow and, broadly speaking, ran parallel to the upper Mississippi when I was a lad. It lay between the land of the hunter and the harvester."

Six of these early stories were collected in *Main-Travelled*

Roads, published in 1891. Two of the stories have Wisconsin settings: ''The Return of the Private,'' about the homecoming of a soldier after the Civil War, and ''Up the Coolly,'' about the conflict between a farmer and his brother, who has gone to the city. Garland became active in the Populist Party, and his political ideas were incorporated in his 1892 novel *A Spoil of Office.* His success as a writer, critic, teacher, and lecturer provided him with some measure of financial security. In 1893 he decided to make his headquarters in Chicago. He was also able to realize his dream of providing a retirement home for his parents, and in that same year he purchased this house in West Salem for his mother and father. The two-story house stood on a five-acre plot. Garland widened the living room and remodeled the kitchen, and in November the elder Garlands moved in.

Garland continued to write extensively. *Rose of Dutcher's Coolly,* his only full-length Wisconsin novel, was published in 1895, and other novels, stories, poems, and articles continued to appear. The profits from his writing enabled him to make more improvements on the house, including the addition of a bay window, enlargment of some of the rooms, and the installation of an indoor bathroom, the first in town.

After an 1898 trip to the Yukon (see Alaska), Garland married, in 1899, Zulime Taft, the sister of the sculptor Lorado Taft. The couple settled in Chicago, but visited the West Salem house frequently, especially in the summer. After the death of Garland's mother, his father moved to a smaller house in town, but the young couple continued to spend their summers in this house, and in 1903 their first child was born here. After his daughter's birth Garland entered upon a major construction project, the building of a fireplace and an outside chimney, described in *A Daughter of the Middle Border.*

Garland and his family (another daughter was born a few years after the first) spent several more summers in the West Salem house. In 1912 a fire gutted a large portion, but Garland had it quickly rebuilt. He spent a final summer in the house after his father's death in 1914, but eventually decided to move to New York City. He purchased a summer home at Lake Onteora, New York, and moved his belongings from the Wisconsin house to his new one. His last years were spent in Los Angeles, California. He died in 1940, and his ashes were returned to West Salem for burial in Neshonoc Cemetery, where a plaque marks the grave site.

In 1972 the Hamlin Garland home was designated a National Historic Landmark. The West Salem Historical Society purchased the house in 1973, began restoration in 1975, and opened it to the public on July 4, 1976. The story of Garland's life here and elsewhere on the frontier is told in his autobiographical Middle Border volumes. *A Son of the Middle Border* (1917) tells of his wandering pioneer family and his boyhood and youth. *A Daughter of the Middle Border* (1921) takes the story up to the death of his father; it concentrates on the lives of his mother, his wife and her family, and his daughters, and contains much material about his life in the West Salem house. The second book was awarded the Pulitzer Prize for biography. Other books in the series are semifictional: *Trail-Makers of the Middle Border* (1926) and *Back-Trailers from the Middle Border* (1927). A historical marker about Hamlin Garland stands at Swarthout Park, just north of West Salem.

WYOMING

Wyoming's primary tourist attractions are natural, with Yellowstone and Grand Teton two of the country's most popular national parks. John Muir's *Our National Parks* is fine background reading. A more recent volume on the natural history of the state is *Wapiti Wilderness* (1966) by Margaret and Olaus Murie, which has beautiful and scientifically accurate descriptions of the wildlife of the Grand Tetons and also gives an account of modern-day life in Jackson Hole.

It is interesting to read of the mountain men and fur trappers who first penetrated the wilderness of Wyoming. The first was John Colter, for whom Colter Bay in the Grand Tetons is named. A member of the Lewis and Clark expedition, he left the party on the return trip in order to trap and discovered a gloomy area of foul-smelling geysers that came to be known as Colter's Hell; he is believed to have reached the headwaters of the Green River and later explored the Yellowstone region. When he went back to St. Louis in 1810 his stories of steaming geysers and boiling springs were at first not believed. *John Colter: His Years in the Rockies* by Burton Harris is a good book on the intrepid explorer.

The overland part of John Jacob Astor's American Fur Company expedition passed through Wyoming in 1811. This journey is chronicled in Washington Irving's *Astoria, or, Anecdotes of an Enterprise Beyond the Rocky Mountains* (see Astoria, Oregon). Irving followed up this book with *The Rocky Mountains, or, Scenes, Incidents and Adventures in the Far West* (1837), later reprinted under the title *The Adventures of Captain Bonneville;* this was based on the journals of Captain B. L. E. Bonneville, who traced a route to the Green River and set up in the fur trade.

Bernard DeVoto's *Across the Wide Missouri,* which won the Pulitzer Prize for history in 1948, is about the Rocky Mountain fur trade and its role in the opening of the West.

Jim Bridger was perhaps the greater mountain man of all (Fort Bridger, Bridger-Teton National Forest, Bridger Lake, and Bridger's Pass are named for him). Bridger was a colorful character who flourished in the 1830s and 1840s. He served as a scout and trailblazer for exploration parties and is credited with the discovery of sections of what is now Yellowstone National Park. There is a museum at **Fort Bridger State Historic Site** at the town of Fort Bridger, with the partially restored fort, established as a trading post by Bridger in 1843. Demonstrations of pioneer crafts are given in the summer (open daily in summer 8–6, shorter hours spring and fall; free). Stanley Vestal's *Jim Bridger, Mountain Man* is the best work about this fascinating personality. Vestal is also the author of *Mountain Men,* which deals with Colter, Bridger, and other early explorers of the Rockies like William Sublette, Jedediah Smith, and Jim Beckwourth. The last has been called "the most celebrated liar on the early frontier"; the tradition of embroidering tales of exploration and adventure is a great one in Western folklore, and probably had its origins with these men. A classic account of this era is *Journal of a Trapper* by Osborne Russell, a contemporary of Bridger and Smith.

An important firsthand account of early exploration and travel in Wyoming is John C. Frémont's *Report of the Exploring Expedition to the Rocky Mountains in the Year 1842 . . .* (published in 1845). Frémont, the "Great Pathfinder" (see California), was sent by the U.S. Government to survey the route from the Mississippi as far as the South Pass, the opening in the Rockies through which thousands of emigrants were to pass on the Oregon Trail. On this journey he reached the summit of what is now known as Frémont Peak, the second highest point in the Wind River Mountains.

In the mid-nineteenth century the West attracted a seeming flood of well-to-do European visitors who on returning home wrote their travel reminiscences. One of the more interesting and talented of these was the Earl of Dunraven, who spent several weeks hunting and sightseeing in Yellowstone in the summer of 1874. In his book *The Great Divide* he describes his awe when on attaining the summit of Mount Washburn he views far below him the streams flowing in different directions, some feeding the great rivers to the Pacific, others the Missouri and ultimately the Mississippi.

After the fur trappers came the westward migration of the pioneers and the beginnings of the cattle industry. The first important writing about the opening of the pioneer roads is *The Oregon Trail* by Francis Parkman (see Fort Laramie). Emerson Hough's novel *The Covered Wagon* (1922) is about a wagon train of 1848 on the Oregon Trail. Hough's contemporary Owen Wister wrote what is probably the archetype of all Westerns, *The Virginian,* which takes place in and around Medicine Bow (which see). Two other early popular writers of Westerns also set a number of their stories in the cow country of Wyoming: William MacLeod Raine wrote *Wyoming: Story of the Outdoor West* (1908), and Zane Grey wrote *Wyoming.* Grey's *Western Union,* about the construction of telegraph lines, is also set largely in Wyoming and has scenes in Fort Bridger; *The U.P. Trail* is about the building of the Union Pacific Railroad across Wyoming in the 1860s. Among more recent writing, the following are notable: *Shane,* by Jack Schaefer, made into a famous movie, is a novel about homesteaders in Wyoming in the 1890s. Frederick Manfred's *Riders of Judgment* is a novel about the bloody wars between the cattle barons and the small ranchers in the late nineteenth century. Larry McMurtry has written a novel entitled *Leaving Cheyenne.*

The first Wyoming writer to gain a national reputation was Bill Nye (1850–96), who came to frontier Wyoming in 1876 and began working on the Laramie *Daily Sentinel* and the Laramie *Boomerang* writing humorous columns characterized by exaggeration and good-natured satire. He later became a platform lecturer with James Whitcomb Riley and became a millionaire from his writings before he died at too early an age. His pieces have been collected in the recently published volumes *Bill Nye's Western Humor* (1968) and *The Best of Bill Nye's Humor* (1973).

Struthers Burt (1882–1954) was one of the better-known Wyoming authors. An Easterner, he spent summers on his Wyoming ranch with his wife Katherine Newlin Burt, also a writer. Among his novels with Wyoming settings are *Chance Encounters* and *The Delectable Mountains; Powder River Let 'er*

Buck is nonfiction. *John O'May and Other Stories* contains short works about Wyoming, and *The Diary of A Dude Wrangler* is autobiographical. Katherine Burt wrote *The Branding Iron* and *Men of Moon Mountain,* among others. Ted Olson is a poet who is a native of Laramie. He was awarded the Younger Poets' prize by *Poetry* magazine in 1928 and has since published poems widely. In 1973 he published *Ranch on the Laramie,* a reminiscence of his boyhood on a Wyoming ranch in the early twentieth century.

The **Western History Research Center** (Coe Library) of the University of Wyoming in **Laramie** has exhibits on Western history and literature, including rare books relating to the West (the library is open to the general public, early morning until late night except academic holidays).

Fort Laramie

Fort Laramie National Historic Site. 2½ miles west of town of Fort Laramie (not to be confused with Laramie). Daily, winter 8–4:30, summer 7–7; closed Christmas and New Year's Day. Free.

In 1846, at the age of twenty-three, shortly after graduating from Harvard, Francis Parkman, scion of a wealthy Boston family, headed west to do research on the Indians of the Plains. He got as far as Kansas City by railroad, stagecoach, and steamboat, and then started out with his guide, Henry Chatillon, a trapper who was familiar with the Oglala Sioux, on horseback along the trail across Nebraska and Wyoming that was being used by emigrants to Oregon. He eventually arrived at Fort Laramie, which was then not a military establishment but a post for fur traders and for covered-wagon pioneers. During his approximately six-month sojourn in Wyoming Parkman became intimate with the local Indians and observed their way of life at first hand. In *The Oregon Trail* (full title: *The California and Oregon Trail: Being Sketches of Prairie and Rocky Mountain Life*), published in 1849, the classic account of the newly opening West, Parkman combines an exciting narrative with a vivid description of the trappers, traders, Indians, and emigrants on the frontier. He writes extensively of life at Fort Laramie:

> Looking back, after the expiration of a year, upon Fort Laramie and its inmates, they seem less like a reality than like some fanciful picture of the olden time; so different was the scene from any which this tamer side of the world can present. Tall Indians, enveloped in their white buffalo-robes, were striding across the area or reclining at full length on the low roofs of the buildings which enclosed it. Numerous squaws, gayly bedizened, sat grouped in front of the rooms they occupied; their mongrel offspring, restless and vociferous, rambled in every direction through the fort; and the trappers, traders, and engagés of the establishment were busy at their labor or their amusements.

At the time, the Indians, although warring among themselves, were on reasonably good terms with the white traders (many of them Frenchmen from Canada) of the area. But Parkman realized that the Indian way of life he observed would soon disappear as the waves of westward migration swelled and the Indians were overwhelmed by "civilization" and military force.

Fort Laramie, as already mentioned, was a fur-trading post and emigrants' way station in 1846. The Marcus Whitman party had stopped here in 1836 en route to Oregon Territory (see Walla Walla, Washington), and later the first Mormon party visited on their way to Utah. In 1849 Fort Laramie was bought by the U.S. Government and was transformed into an army post to help protect emigrants from hostile Indians. The army built many structures, and in the present restoration of the fort the oldest buildings are actually ones dating from 1849, when the military takeover occurred. The necessity for Fort Laramie waned in the 1870s after Indian hostilities had been settled either by treaty or by force, and the fort was abandoned in 1890, left to fall into decay for almost fifty years, until it was named a National Historical Site in 1938. The restored buildings include a trader's store, the lieutenant colonel's quarters, "Old Bedlam" (bachelor officers' quarters), post surgeon's quarters, and captain's quarters, all, however, dating from the period after Francis Parkman was here. Many descriptive and historical books and pamphlets are for sale at the shop here.

Other sites of interest in the area are the **Scotts Bluff National Monument** (55 miles southwest, in Nebraska), a pioneer's landmark; **Register Cliff** (3 miles southeast of Guernsey, Wyoming, 650 feet south of the North Platte River), where thousands of emigrants wrote their names on the chalk face; and **Oregon Trail ruts,** visible about 2 miles south of Guernsey (turn south on Main Street and follow signs). The nearby towns of **Guernsey** and **Torrington** both have museums with exhibits about the emigrants.

Medicine Bow

Owen Wister was a well-born gentleman from Philadelphia, the grandson of the great English actress Fanny Kemble. He had gone to Harvard (where he became friends with Theodore Roosevelt, who was two years ahead of him), was musically talented, and had traveled through Europe, where he had played his own composition for Franz Lizst. This well-to-do, sophisticated Easterner might seem an unlikely person to have invented the Western romance, but it was he who became the author of *The Virginian* (1902), the prototype for the thousands of Westerns published afterward.

In 1885, at the age of twenty-five, Wister's health broke, and he went to stay at a friend's ranch in Wyoming at the advice of a family friend, Dr. S. Weir Mitchell (who was also a well-known novelist). From the first he kept a journal—these journals and his letters have been published in *Owen Wister Out West: His Journals and Letters* (1958), edited by his daughter Fanny Kemble Wister—and recorded that "the air is delicious" and that he could not say "how extraordinary and beautiful the valleys we've been going through are." (The original journals are now in the Owen Wister Room of the library of the University of Wyoming in Laramie.) At the ranch he hunted, saw calves branded, and observed and took part in cattle roundups. The nearest town with a railroad was Medicine Bow, a nineteen-hour ride away, where he collected freight for the ranch. Medicine Bow, the only town mentioned by name in *The Virginian,* consisted at the time of a total of twenty-nine buildings; Wister wrote: "This place is called a town. 'Town' will do very well until the language stretches itself and takes in a new word that fits."

Wister went back east that autumn to enter Harvard Law School, from which he graduated in 1888; he was admitted to the Philadelphia bar in 1890. But he continued to spend his summers in Wyoming.

In *Roosevelt, The Story of a Friendship* Wister relates how he began writing stories of the West. One autumn evening in 1891, "fresh from Wyoming," he was dining at his Philadelphia club with Walter Furness, who also loved the West.

> Why wasn't some Kipling saving the sage-brush for American literature, before the sage-brush and all that it signified went the way of the California forty-niner, went the way of the Mississippi steam-boat, went the way of everything? Roosevelt had seen the sage-brush true, had felt its poetry; and also Remington, who illustrated his articles so well. But what was fiction doing, fiction, the only thing that has always outlived fact? Must it be perpetual tea-cups? Was Alkali Ike in the comic papers the one figure which the jejune American imagination, always at full-cock to banter or to brag, could discern in that epic which was being lived at a gallop out in the sage-brush? "To hell with tea-cups and the great American laugh!" we two said, as we sat dining at the club. The claret had been excellent.
>
> "Walter, I'm going to try it myself!" I exclaimed to Walter Furness. "I'm going to start this minute."

He went up to the library of the club and began writing his first Western story, "Hank's Woman," a tragic tale of the mistreatment of a woman by her brutal husband in a Wyoming mining camp. It was published in *Harper's Magazine,* which also published his subsequent stories, including the Lin McLean stories, collected in *Lin McLean* (1897).

In 1902 came *The Virginian.* It is set in the cattle country around Medicine Bow. The unnamed cowboy hero of the novel is a real human being, not the rough stick figure of the dime-novel Western fiction that has preceded this book. He can be gentle but he can also be hard with his enemies; he occasionally gets drunk, but he is highly competent at his job. The heroine is the archetypal New England schoolmarm, with whom he falls in love. He lives by the code of the West, and has no qualms about lynching his former friend Steve when Steve is discovered to be a rustler. At the beginning of the book a confrontation takes place over a game of cards in a saloon between the Virginian and the villain, a drifter and rustler named Trampas. Trampas makes the mistake of calling the Virginian a "son-of-a-_____" (sic). The Virginian draws his pistol, holds it unaimed on top of the table, and utters the immortal line, "When you call me that, *smile!*" At the end of the story, Trampas and the Virginian have a showdown on the day before the Virginian's wedding to Molly Wood, the schoolteacher, and Trampas is (of course) killed.

Wister drew on his experiences in the cattle country of Wyoming for background material, and although the character of the hero is purely fictional and the plot somewhat romantic, many incidents in the book actually occurred, and the details of ranch life are realistic. *The Virginian* was a huge bestseller, and was translated into many languages. The book, for better or worse, established the myth of the Western hero that was to pervade the fiction and film of the newly begun century.

In the center of Medicine Bow is the landmark **Virginian Hotel.** Nearby is a monument to Wister erected in 1939, a year after the author's death.

The **Occidental Hotel** in **Buffalo,** north in Johnson County, with an authentic Old West atmosphere, claims to be the place where the Virginian "got his man."

INDEX

VOLUMES IN THE
AMERICANS-DISCOVER-AMERICA SERIES

Available from your bookseller or from William Morrow & Company, Inc., 6 Henderson Drive, West Caldwell, NJ 07006

Canoeing and Rafting: The Complete Where-to-Go Guide to America's Best Tame and Wild Waters, by Sara Pyle. $5.95

Walking: A Guide to Beautiful Walks and Trails in America, by Jean Calder. $3.95

Skiing USA: A Guide to the Nation's Ski Areas, by Lucy M. Fehr. $4.95

American Travelers' Treasury: A Guide to the Nation's Heirlooms, by Suzanne Lord. $5.95

Traveling with Children in the USA: A Family Guide to Pleasure, Adventure, Discovery, by Leila Hadley. $4.95

A Literary Tour Guide to the United States: Northeast, by Emilie C. Harting. $4.95 Travelflex, $8.95 hardcover

A Literary Tour Guide to the United States: West and Midwest, by Rita Stein. $5.95 Travelflex, $9.95 hardcover

A Literary Tour Guide to the United States: South and Southwest, by Rita Stein. $5.95 Travelflex, $9.95 hardcover

Also available:

The Flag Book of the United States, by Whitney Smith. $5.95 paper, $12.95 hardcover

Volumes in the Americans-Discover-America series are available from your bookseller or from William Morrow & Company, Inc.

When ordering, add 50¢ postage and handling for the first book, plus 25¢ for each additional book. Make checks payable to William Morrow & Company, Inc. (Prices subject to change without notice.)

To: William Morrow & Company, Inc.
6 Henderson Drive
West Caldwell, NJ 07006

Please send me:

Quantity   Price

_____ Canoeing and Rafting: The Complete
Where-to-Go Guide to America's Best
Tame and Wild Waters ($5.95)   _____

_____ Walking: A Guide to Beautiful Walks and
Trails in America ($3.95)   _____

_____ Skiing USA: A Guide to the Nation's Ski
Areas ($4.95)   _____

_____ American Travelers' Treasury: A Guide to
the Nation's Heirlooms ($5.95)   _____

_____ Traveling with Children in the USA: A
Family Guide to Pleasure, Adventure,
Discovery ($4.95)   _____

_____ A Literary Tour Guide to the United States:
Northeast ($4.95 Travelflex, $8.95
hardcover)   _____

_____ A Literary Tour Guide to the United States:
West and Midwest ($5.95 Travelflex, $9.95
hardcover)   _____

_____ A Literary Tour Guide to the United States:
South and Southwest ($5.95 Travelflex,
$9.95 hardcover)   _____

_____ The Flag Book of the United States ($5.95
paper, $12.95 hardcover)   _____

Postage   _____

Sales tax if applicable   _____

Total   _____

NAME

STREET

CITY   STATE   ZIP